# Daniel and Agnes Freeman
## First Homesteaders

# DANIEL AND AGNES FREEMAN

# HOMESTEADERS

*by Beverly S. Kaplan*

*J & L Lee Co.*

ISBN 0-934904-26-X
Previously published by Johnsen Publishing Co.


J & L Lee Co.
Postal Box # 5575
Lincoln, NE  68505

# Dedicated:

To my parents and husband, true champions of democratic liberty; and to my children, Debby, Phoebe, Samuel, and Daniel, apt students of these ideals.

# Contents

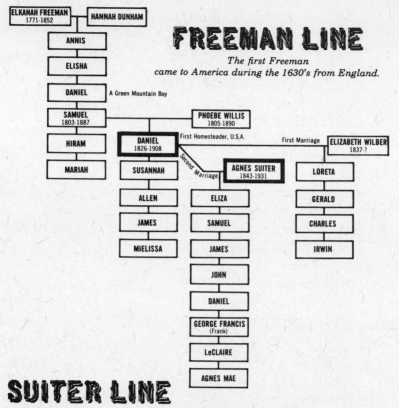

# FREEMAN LINE

*The first Freeman
came to America during the 1630's from England.*

ELKANAH FREEMAN
1771-1852 — HANNAH DUNHAM

ANNIS

ELISHA

DANIEL — A Green Mountain Boy

SAMUEL
1803-1887 — PHOEBE WILLIS
1805-1890

HIRAM

MARIAH

DANIEL
1826-1908 — First Homesteader, U.S.A. — First Marriage — ELIZABETH WILBER
1837-?

Second Marriage — AGNES SUITER
1843-1931

SUSANNAH

ALLEN — ELIZA — LORETA

JAMES — SAMUEL — GERALD

MIELISSA — JAMES — CHARLES

JOHN — IRWIN

DANIEL

GEORGE FRANCIS
(Frank)

LeCLAIRE

AGNES MAE

# SUITER LINE

*No complete genealogical record has been established as yet.*

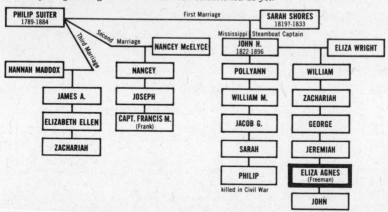

PHILIP SUITER
1789-1884 — First Marriage — SARAH SHORES
1819?-1833

Second Marriage — NANCEY McELYCE

Third Marriage — Mississippi Steamboat Captain
JOHN H.
1822-1896 — ELIZA WRIGHT

HANNAH MADDOX

JAMES A. — NANCEY — POLLYANN — WILLIAM

ELIZABETH ELLEN — JOSEPH — WILLIAM M. — ZACHARIAH

ZACHARIAH — CAPT. FRANCIS M.
(Frank) — JACOB G. — GEORGE

SARAH — JEREMIAH

PHILIP — ELIZA AGNES
(Freeman)

killed in Civil War

JOHN

# List of Illustrations
## BETWEEN PAGES 54 & 55

*Pencil illustrations 3, 4 and 14 and front cover sketch are by Artist Thespa Freeman Stapaules, sister of the Author and also great granddaughter of Daniel and Agnes Freeman.

Editors note—Artist Stapaules is an accomplished Kansas artist. Studied under prominent midwestern artist Karl Mattern. Has displayed her award winning paintings in several states besides Kansas.

# Preface

The Homestead Act epitomized America when it was passed. The people who foresook the established comforts of Eastern law and living to make the Homestead Law a reality typified what the foundation of this nation consisted of. Without men and women willing to tackle the hardships of a pioneer existence and see the struggle through to its end, the nation would still be hovering about the Eastern seaboard.

There was a price these hardy independent people paid for their free soil. It came in the form of hardship, death, deprivation, seeming roughness, uncouthness, and leathering like the soil they inhabited. But to people like Daniel and Agnes Freeman, there was no price too great to pay to bring the American Constitution to flourish upon the prairies. Toughness begot law and order, firmness begot justice. Sometimes, near lynchings, mob action, and ignorance retaliated in cruel ways, but still the price was not too great for these people who innately knew that free soil rendered free soul. Without freedom there was nothing.

Dan and Agnes were true patriots. They were so inculcated with the urgency of freedom that they were ridiculed by those who could not fathom this love of country nor their compassion for truth and justice. To question was to make waves. One who made waves, even among the bolder pioneers, was one to be shunned, to be skeptical of, even though waves would reverberate into the next generation, touch off new waves in another generation and ultimately insure true freedom in the country.

Daniel Freeman was unconventional, bold, and farsighted. One of his most outstanding characteristics was his free thinking. He maintained the Bible was for those who believe in it, he had no objection to this, but he fervently believed it should not be forced upon people who did not want it. True freedom was in the choice, he maintained. He consistently linked his name and efforts with the cause of freedom and frequently declared he was ready to die for this cause he believed in. . . "Free homes for free men, guided by free thoughts, and a clear conscience," summed up his philosophy. This audacious free thinker, sometimes nullified by enemies, fought efforts to subdue and enslave people wherever he could. Never one to demand acceptance of his beliefs by others, he demanded and expected the same privilege from them for himself. The Supreme Court case he brought to separate church and state in Nebraska was a prime example of this belief.

He was a man given to many colorful expletives and adjectival swearing, but who carefully avoided and deplored obscenity. His method of dealing with issues he felt wrong was to teach by object lessons. When a scoundrel did wrong, he set about to teach him a lesson, as in the Court House Square case. The price of the lesson was an inconsiderate, both to himself and his family.

Agnes, though quiet, supported Daniel, his beliefs, and his methods for obtaining justice in the new land. Without her quiet support and unending patience, her fortitude, insight and gentleness, he could not have succeeded.

In August, 1969, twenty five descendants gathered at Homestead National Monument, a national park preserved upon the land of Daniel and Agnes Freeman's original claim, to form the *Descendants of Daniel Freeman and Agnes Suiter Freeman* an organization designed to perpetuate the principles and beliefs in freedom and democracy held by these two sturdy pioneers.

# Acknowledgements

Special appreciation is given to the following people and institutions for their gracious and unstinting help in securing data and information relating to the compilation of this book:

Mrs. Adelaide Freeman Stapaules, Charles R. Quackenbush, Mrs. Gladys Freeman Bueoy, Mrs. Mabel Carre Carpenter, Mrs. Maude Freeman.

The Nebraska State Historical Society, and their staff; Dean Brandt, clerk of the District Court, Gage County, Nebraska and his staff; the Beatrice Public Library; The Beatrice Daily Sun; Homestead National Monument and staff; and the Descendants of Daniel Freeman and Agnes Suiter Freeman Organization.

Special appreciation is here given to the many people who volunteered time for interviews, bits of information, letters and documents of value.

Reverent respect to the memory of those beloved people who gave much time and thought to a young inquisitive girl many years ago when the nucleus of this biography was first being formed is hereby acknowledged—especially to that of my late grandfather, Samuel Freeman. Others include Agnes Freeman Quackenbush, Verna Taylor, LeClaire Freeman, Eliza Freeman Carre.

I am most grateful to my mother, who provided letters, personal knowledge, and stacks of data collected by her many years ago, when the Freeman family was young and flourishing.

For the hundreds of private letters, papers, and documents from personal collections along with personal contributions so generously given by the many descendants of the Freeman family for this work, I am deeply indebted.

For editorial assistance, my thanks to Linda L. Baker.

# Introduction

The great granddaughter of Daniel and Agnes Freeman, Beverly Stapaules Kaplan, author, college instructor, former mail carrier, mother, inventor, carpenter, farmer, is the epitomy of the pioneer spirit as it survives in this country today. During our short acquaintance, I have found her to be an extraordinary woman; liberated in every true sense of the word, yet kind, warm and intently concerned with preserving her own identity in a complex world and in securing the right of each of us to do the same.

More is reflected in this story of Daniel and Agnes Freeman than the justification of the claim to Homestead No. 1. The courage, stamina and straightforward honesty of the people who built the country West of the Missouri is delineated here. This book is not an attempt to glorify the Freeman family or the people who settled alongside them near Beatrice, Nebraska; it is an attempt to bring to life the spirit which carried the early homesteaders through drought, depression and disease and still allowed them to recite a good story or lend an ailing neighbor a hand, seldom brooding over their own losses.

Nebraska was a semi-arid desert land when Daniel Freeman first looked upon it. All of us, it would seem, should think favorably of that Freeman who, gazing at stringy buffalo grass, saw a land blossoming into the lush, green agricultural center of the nation.

The 1800's were hard years and Nebraska a harsh territory. The men and women who settled here were ordinary people who had left the comforts of warm homes to take up their personal struggles with the land. They were, morally and ethically, no better or worse than those of us who live on that same land today, but they seemed to merge with the soil and draw strength of spirit and purpose from its resiliency and resistance to the plow.

This is the story Beverly Kaplan has told. I believe it relates the real drama and significance of the Westward movement and reassures all of us of the heritage left us by our own pioneer ancestors.

*Linda L. Baker*

# I

# The Prairie
_____  1862

*Nebrathka*, the land of "flat water" to the Otoe, was no more than an inhabitable desert territory to the Easterner. It was governed by a wilderness of tall grasses, snorting herds of brown bison and mule-eared jackrabbits. Slinking, yellow-brown coyotes and grey timber wolves marshalled the plains from draws and ravines in yapping barking vigilante packs.

The Otoe, Cheyenne, Sioux and Omaha tribes padded from hunting ground to hunting ground. Their only perceivable imprints upon the virgin prairie were the charred spots from their campfires and the flattened grasses trailing their migrations. The rains and wind, sometimes gentle, sometimes fierce and treacherous, soon washed away the meager signs of the campsites and the dew from the night sprung the grasses upright again. Searing heat in the summer, frigid winters, and wanton prairie fires dancing wildly like the heels of Satan across the virgin breast of the land could not subdue the resiliency of this Nebraska Soil.

While men in France and Spain played games of ownership with this vast territory, shunting the spoils back and forth, the land dutifully bloomed in the Spring and withered in the Autumn, unmindful of its destiny. Untamed and free, it was like the elk, the deer, and the prairie chicken that it nurtured.

Politics caught up with geography. In 1803, through the Louisiana Purchase, a union between this territory and America was legalized. It was the beginning of a political union between this land and the white man. Between this vast, open prairie and the Indians and buffalo, the single unity was forever severed.

The eastern slopes of the Nebraska territory that bordered along the hustling Missouri River were heavy with timber. Oak, cottonwood, and willows hovered gaunt and gray above the bubbling waterway. Counties later designated Pawnee, Nemaha, Johnson, Richardson, and Gage made up the southeasternmost area of the territory. The bluffs along the Missouri gave way to rolling hills, rivers, and creeks westward to Gage county. Valuable timber followed and clung to the banks of the winding streams. Mammoth layers of yellowed limestone lay exposed along the gorges of the *Nee-haun-chee-toe*, the Big Blue River, as the Otoe had named it.

These were the hunting grounds of the Otoe and Pawnee, and to the Sioux further to the west of the *Nee-haun-chee-toe*. Beyond the Sioux, westward, the Cheyenne roamed.

The Otoe tribe clung to the Big Blue River, its uplands and lowlands. After a treaty was signed in 1854, they lived peacefully next to the Missouri tribe on a reservation in the southern part of what is now Gage county. Here they were content to hunt, fish, and barter with the white man who was beginning to enter the territory. This was the hunting ground of the Otoe where their Waconda breathed the spirit of life into the blowing grasses and the running deer. Waconda spat the fire into the lightning and stamped the thunder into the clouds and put the spirit wherever life was. It was their religion, simple and unfettered as the life they led. It was a belief that the white man, for lack of depth and understanding, had to qualify as did Major A. L. Green, later appointed Indian Affairs Agent to the Otoe. "Waconda was their religion, if it can be called that," he wrote.

It was 1862 and a mild June. The wind southwesterly and lazy. Only the lush grasses, shoulder high on a horse, worked before the breeze in the lowlands. On the uplands, between dry draws and ravines that exposed their colored earths, the thick short kinky buffalo grass choked out all other vegetation. The pale blue Spider Wort and the pink wild roses gently scented the air above the rolling swells and undulations of the prairie.

Dan drew Prince to a walk. He crossed his arms over the butt of his Springfield dangling from the saddle holster. It was easier on the horse—a hell of a lot easier on the man when the horse walked. But who had time for easier? He took the rein again and nudged the black stallion. The animal was lathering between the hind legs and hadn't drunk since the last buffalo wallow. There had been precious little there in the hoof tracks for a horse to drink. Even so, he had to get to Beatrice before dark. Too many Cheyenne on the war path along the Republican. He'd seen enough of their hell-raising around Fort Kearney.

He'd seen enough, but there would be more. There had been since he enlisted at the outbreak of the war. He'd enlisted in the 17th Illinois infantry, but there were too many men. Because of his six years experience with the Pinkertons before he entered the army, he was whisked quickly into the Secret Service.

Now that he was off duty, he pushed the horse eastward relentlessly. His long legs bobbed time easily with the gallop. Prince was a big horse, but the man astride him seemed disproportionately tall and gangly.

As he rode down hills and over them, his wild black beard tangled with the wind. "Ten miles. Maybe fifteen, Prince." He said roughly to encourage his horse. An ear flicked backward to catch the sound, the gait was uninterrupted.

At the top of the rise he saw three Indians busy stripping the carcass of a deer on the hillside. He watched them while he continued straight ahead. Otoe or Pawnee, likely. They were too preoccupied to look or to care as the tall man on the black horse passed them.

Evening shadows crept behind the trees and danced across the clear water bouncing down Cub Creek. Little eddies and washes formed around Prince's knees and played up against his hocks as he drank. Dan listened to the gurgle of the water and the chilling scream of the night hawk overhead. Phoebes twittered and gossiped in the big oak on the far bank. The black eyes twinkled and the big hand reached out and stroked the tired horse's neck gently, silently.

They followed the creek a ways before they found a bench on the bank to climb out. There was a stirring in the man as he drew out of the timber on to the flat lowland with five varieties of sweet grasses growing so lush and tall Prince reared his head in protest as he wedged his way through it. Grass and water and wood. Not too far from Beatrice. On the peak of the east hill he surveyed the land he had just passed through. The stirring again. Off to the right, a little log cabin sat. What a home this would make if the homestead bill they'd been haggling over would ever be signed. But someone was luckier than he, they already had a squatters shack on it. Angered at this sight, he bridled Prince abruptly and shouted, "Get the Goddamned hell outta here." The startled animal moved obediently.

The Big Blue stopped them abruptly. In the twighlight, Dan could make out a little settlement across the river. Once again Prince entered the water, this time up to his belly and swimming in the deeper spots.

"Anybody home?" The tall man with the bedeviled whiskers boomed. A small, balding man, bathed in sleepy sweat, rose from a make-shift cot in the corner of the room and came up to the counter.

"Got any place for a man to sleep and lodge his horse?" The little man nodded.

"Freeman, Daniel Freeman." He answered the other's querie.

By the time Daniel had stabled his horse, an interested

crowd had gathered around him with questions of the Indian situation to the west, how far away the Cheyenne were, and if a railroad, "is really gonna come out hea' to Nebrisky?"

Freeman told them all he knew of the Indian situation from his scouting trip.

"You a scout, mister? Which side?"

"Union, damnit!" Dan spat.

"You see any redskin heathens clos't by hea'?"

Dan's eyes blazed as he glowered at the man that had asked him which side he was on. "Hell yes. I saw three and they said they was out lookin' for a little son-of-a-bitch cuss just like you."

The men guffawed and Dan turned around with a merry twinkle in his deep black eyes. "That crick west of the Blue, what is it?"

"Cub. You must mean Cub Crick, hunh?"

"Fixin' to get a homestead, hunh?"

"Maybe."

"Why not? This gotta be a helluva good soil rount here. No better place to settle in the worl'. Now that the Homestead Act passed, ever son-of-a-gun an' his ol' blue tick'll fer sure start headin' out this way."

Dan stopped and his great frame jerked toward the man. "You say the homestead act passed? When?"

"Fer sure it did. They say ol' Abe signed her the twentieth day a' May. We jist heard on it. Don't take ee-fect till the first day a' Janiary—that'll be '63."

That forest of grass on Cub Creek—the stirring again. God-a-mighty if a man could just get a fist of that. It could make a man forget the hurts and heal the wounds of his pride and soul. He'd almost forgotten Elizabeth. Flying across the prairie on the back of an old army steed a man could almost out run his feelings until he stopped. Then, there it was again—big, black, gnawing. His country and his home were both dismally divided. He saw the faces of his

three young ones cast against the background of swaying
grasses. If not for the little ones. But— forget, forget. It's
done, she's gone. A new start, that's what a man needs, a
new start in a new country.

He'd started fresh from medical school in Ottawa, Illinois
with Elizabeth beside him. "The greatest thing you can do
for your fellow man is to be able to heal his sick body,"
they'd taught him at the Cincinnati School of Eclectic
Medicine. He had believed that. Now his own spirit was
wounded and needed healing, but there was no healer
except time.

Morning came and found Daniel brooding astride his
black horse on the hilltop above Cub Creek. The morning
dew from wading the prairie grasses trickled down the
horse's flanks and puddled beneath him. Smoke drifted
softly from the chimney of the cabin. Yes, he would go
visit the man in the cabin.

"Come in stranger. Nancey's got the chickory hot. Come
set a spell. We don't get visitors often. What brings ya' into
this country, man? M' name's Job Harris, this here's
Nancey." The grizzled man jerked his thumb toward his
wife.

Dan took the rough work worn hand and made himself
known.

"Dan'l Freeman, hunh? Where from? Did you know
William and Sarey Freeman back in Ohio?"

"I was born in Preble County in Ohio, but my Pa moved
us to New York when I was only a year old. Was there 9
years, then he and Ma took us on to Illinois. Don't know
who the hell is still there, if anybody."

Nancey's face dropped.

"We be from Ohio way. Jist a shade over a year here
now. Nancey, she don't like it much. Misses her kin
sumpin' awful." Harris sadly rubbed his coarse stubble.
"But God, a man could make this soil do fer 'im effen he
had time." He brightened. "Don't need no money, hardly.

Jest time, an' belly guts, an' a heap a' strong back. Yessir."
He glanced guiltily at Nancey. "That's all a man needs." He
rasped one thick hand against the other and avoided
looking at Nancey again. "I promised Nancey meat for
dinner. Welcome to come a' hunt with me, Dan'l."

The men struck out for the prairie south of the cabin.
Lots of antelope between the draws there, Harris had
promised.

"See that big buck down that draw?" Dan asked.

Harris nodded.

"You go on down this draw, I'll come in from the other
end. We'll sure as hell have him trapped."

At the point of meeting, Dan came upon Harris, head
down, stumbling along with his gun under his arm. No
antelope was in sight. "Why in hell didn't you shoot one of
them when they scattered up the bank?" he demanded.

Harris looked up startled, "Oh, I didn't even see 'em. I
was thinking about the awful scoldin' Nancey give me this
morning." He pushed the floppy felt hat onto the back of
his head and scratched through greasy hair. "She's a mighty
homesick woman."

"How much you want for your squatter's claim?" Dan
never hedged with preliminaries.

The men faced each other on the south slope. The
breeze was gentle and cool. Harris began to toe the butt of
the blue stem with his boot worn red. Dan waited, feet
apart.

"Nancey's so homesick and wants to go back to Ohio so
bad to her folks I'd take any means of gettin' there."

"Would a yoke of oxen and a cart be fair means?"

"It be fair means an' more," he grinned. They grasped
hands on the bargain.

Dan returned late the next afternoon with a yoke of two
year old bulls hitched to a cart. He'd had to search as far
as Blue Springs for them. He stayed to help Harris pack the
cart. Nancey stepped lightly and her spirits were buoyant.

The cook stove? Leave it for Dan'l and the
lady he's goin' to bring to this country. She'll
bake their first biscuits and fry her first grouse
on it. The mattresses? Hell, no. Only make
bedding for the mice and rats whilst nobody's
here. Empty the ticking. Leave the ticking if you
want, but empty it. Leave the table. Bench too.
Ain't nothin' but hewed logs. All I want's to git
back to O-hi-ee. This be Nathan Blakely. He from
up-crick. Helluva good man. Could you borry my
new cook stove? Hell yes! Keep it till I get back
from war. I'll mash the rebs—I'll mash 'em god-
dam good.

Jeez-us! To get back and taste that O-hi-ee
made apple butter. I'll eat it 'till I'm full up on
it. Then I'll eat some more. You, Dan'l Freeman,
you man of men. Me'n Nancey'll not soon fergit.
Fair means and them some, Dan'l. Giddap. Hya,
hya, hya.

Dan staked out the best one hundred and sixty acres of
bottom land along Cub Creek in the form of a *T*. He
worked quickly, but carefully. He had already lost three
days of his furlough, and he wanted to get back home to
Abingdon, Illinois to see his folks, Samuel and Phoebe
Freeman and brother James. James, fifteen years younger
than Dan was just graduated from Abingdon College and
betrothed to a likeable girl who had shared a classroom
with Bill Cody back in LeClaire, Iowa. James had met
Agnes Suiter at Abingdon College and they had graduated
together. Samuel and Phoebe Freeman doted upon their
youngest son as did his elder brother Dan. He was known
to be "a young man of uncommon brilliance," a poet of
sorts. In the heat of August and the heat of a civil conflict,
James had signed up with the 83rd Illinois Volunteers. He
would be going to Fort Donelson along the Cumberland

River in Tennessee. Agnes went back patiently to LeClaire to start her trousseau and her teaching and to wait for her "Cousin James' "[1] first furlough, when they would be married.

Dan, still heavy in heart over Elizabeth, set out again for the southwest and further orders from his Commanding General Pleasonton. Once again Samuel and Phoebe Freeman's house was lone and empty.

A Secret Service Agent and a Scout travel far, alone, and often disguised. Deep into southern territory, into every state in the confederacy, Dan was sent to ferret positions and numbers of troops and bring back information. With a crutch and cane as disguise, he was detailed to Richmond with a message to General Pleasonton. A ride with a carter and a swim across the Potomac River with his clothes tied in a bundle to the back of his head accomplished his mission. Back in the middle country. This time to the hills of western Missouri after Quantrill and his marauding bushwhackers. He was detailed one hundred men to flush Quantrill and his men from hiding. After a tip from a Missourian that Quantrill was hiding in a nearby gulley, and a plea never to tell who told him or "it's all my hide is wuth', Dan took his men and waited out. It was Quantrill's camp, but the elusive bushwhacker either escaped or was not in camp when the attack was made.

The following months were fear ridden; filled with gloom, despair, victory and death. Always the death. Scarcely a home was untouched by the shroud of this black scourage during the Civil War. The Freeman family was no exception. The jolt of death fell upon Samuel and Phoebe's home in November, 1862. Their beloved James, so recently a graduate, so recently a volunteer, dead of black measles at Fort Donelson. The girl he was to marry was summoned

---

[1] "Cousin" was the strongest endearment proper young ladies allowed themselves to use in reference to the man they loved.

to their home for comfort and to comfort them. Where was the God the churchmen preached of so blithely. They recalled the cruel hoax played upon them in earlier years when the little girl given to baptism in the icy creek died of pneumonia. Where was this God that they say cares? Where is He when thousands of young men are fighting brother against brother and dying in their tracks? Where is this God who lets men kill? It was a sorrow so heavy that they would never again stand straight beneath its weight. It was a sorrow that would scar the girl, Agnes, all her life.

Daniel was needed. The only living son left. He would come as quickly as his mission ended.

Dan had known Agnes through brother Jim, but not well. She was deeply hurt, but she bore her pain well. She was a lady. She comforted his mother who saw the end of all life and effort. Slowly Agnes was able to prevail upon the mother of her beloved "Cousin Jim" to again take up with the living.

The sorrow in Daniel was deep and his pity for this young woman was great. One hurt comes to rest beside another, and another and the scar it leaves helps to protect against the next hurt—and time, with its magical powers, heals all.

# II

# Settling Down

## 1863 — 1865

The gloom of death pervaded the entire nation. The invasion of Kentucky, the battle of Perryville, Antietam, and the Union cried: conscription, conscription. It was no longer a battle of young men, but of old men, boys, entire families.

In Missouri, a push was on to back Confederate Sterling Price to the Gulf of Mexico if necessary to defeat him. His bushwhackers were busy looting and burning the contents of Union supply wagons. Winter gripped the nation and it was finally accepted that the three month war was going to be a lengthy struggle, with collosal and unimpeded bitterness.

Dan was again sent into Missouri to help stop the destruction of Union supply wagons. In LeClaire, Agnes settled into a routine of teaching and sewing to help crowd out her thoughts of James. She read her first letter from Dan in December twighlight and marveled that he found time to share her grief. He spoke briefly of a homestead in the Nebraska territory he would file claim to if he could manage the leave from his duties. He mentioned neither James nor Elizabeth by name, his words to Agnes seemed to grow out of their common grief.

The leave was granted, sooner than Dan anticipated, in the form of a detour from Fort Leavenworth. The final stipulation was that he report in St. Louis for new orders not later than January 2, 1863. This gave him just enough time to ride from Fort Leavenworth to Brownville, Nebraska Territorial Land Office and on to St. Louis. He had not considered the holiday season and made his arrival

at Brownville on December 31, 1862, New Year's eve. He
arrived after dark and secured quarters for himself and his
horse. An impatient man when he had things to do and
bound by deadlines, he was ready to attend to business and
be gone.

There was a flurry of hoop skirts among the few, mostly
bawdy, women there and a shuffle of fresh blacked boots
among mud-caked ones as the New Year's evening wore on.
The spirit was holiday and the war temporarily remote to
most of the townspeople and the few homestead seekers.
Whiskey brightened the gloom for some, but they all
attended the New Year's Ball, shuffling and scraping and
tripping to the time of *Buffalo Girls* and *The Arkansas
Traveler*. Dan went too, impatient with the gaiety and his
delay. He sat the dances out at first, quietly cursing his
luck. At the insistence of a booming jovial voice from
behind a red bushy beard, he reluctantly joined in one
Virginia Reel. His great military frame glided gracefully
through the do-si-dos. Black scrutinizing eyes, framed by
the wild black beard, danced time with his feet. The reel
ended and he moved swiftly to the benches along the wall.
"Who is the land office man? Is he here tonight?" He
confronted the man on the bench.

"Well, I know the assistant."

"I've come a long way to file claim to a parcel of land.
If you could see your way clear to help me..." He
explained his plight.

"You hafta talk with Jim Bedford, he's the assistant.
Jamison's outta town. He's the registrar."

"Where do I find this Jim Bedford?" Strains of *Turkey
in the Straw* yanked from the resilient gut of the banjo
strings competed with the zee-zwa-ing of the two fiddles to
be heard. The shuffle, the stomp, the scrape. The room was
small and crowded. Hickory shirts in blues and checks,
calico and gingham, the floor was a whirl of colored motion.

The red bearded man brushed his ear from the tickle of Dan's beard. "Up the hill," he shouted. "I'll take you." He motioned for Dan to follow.

On the hillside, in his half dugout, half cabin, James Bedford listened intently to the soldier's story. "A damned predicament, indeed."

"I wouldn't mind," Dan said, "but I'm due to go East again and when I could get back here hell and damnation only knows. I'm afraid somebody will take my claim since it has a cabin on it, and a little ground turned. I've put money out already on it. I'll have no damn protection if I don't lock it tight now."

Jim Bedford nodded. He handed Dan's army orders back to him. "Tomorrow's a holiday, too, ya know. New Year's day and the land office won't be open till eight o'clock come the second."

Dan was serious, politely insistent. "I know this is asking a lot, but I'm a secret service agent and I'm giving all I've got to this land too."

Jim Bedford nodded again. Snatches of *Nellie Blye* jerked in agonizing spasms toward them as they proceeded toward the land office.

Cheers and the report from a Sharp's Carbine announced the arrival of the New Year, 1863. Dan drew the blotter from his signature and pushed the claim papers and the fourteen dollars filing fee for his homestead on Cub Creek towards Jim Bedford. "They're raisin' one helluva ruckus with that carbine. Goddamn, if I didn't have to commence at five in the morning, I'd kick up my heels and snort like hell too." His long arm shot across the table and grasped Bedford's hand in grateful appreciation. He would not waste a moment. On the next carbine report he drew the blanket over his fully clothed body, grateful for the shelter of the hotel room. Five o'clock would arrive early enough and St. Louis was a jolting weary ride against time.

What America needed this January 1, 1863 was a

powerful emetic that would purge the hate, fear, and
weariness from its saddened countryside scarred with
carrion, conflagrations, and stench. It needed a hypodermic
of hope that would carry beyond the disease of the prison
camps and the bellies sunken with hunger. It was a time
when Abraham Lincoln's people could neither retreat nor
advance. It was with perception that he announced, "In
regards to the Homestead law . . . I am in favor of cutting
the wild lands into parcels, so that every poor man may
have a home." And so this day the Homestead law became
officially effective. He advanced upon this same day the
Emancipation Proclamation. All men could be free with a
chunk of land to do it on, the law said. With this stimulus,
the black days of the Union were slowly dispelled and the
Civil War's end more clearly defined.

Agnes Suiter read the news of Dan's filing. The registrar
at Brownville was a fine fellow and they got the job done
only after a hell of a time. Agnes winced as she read this
last part of the letter. Knowing how Daniel would have said
it if he were speaking, she smiled—this was mild. It would
make a fine home someday when the Union wiped the
renegades from the continent, he continued. There would
come a time for living.

Peace and rest, thought Agnes, that is what the nation
needed. Peace for Daniel, perhaps, but never rest. Of this
she was quite sure. He was a man who hungered for
answers to unanswerable questions. A restless man who
must always be on the move, never idle. A man seeking,
feeling, probing but—nevertheless a very unusual man, she
sighed.

There was an accelerated flow of "private notes" between Daniel and Agnes. Foresight prodded Dan to think
of the future and forget his unhappy past. His next leave
found him back in Ottawa, Illinois arranging for the divorce
from the Elizabeth Wilbur, who had deserted him four
years before and taken his children where he could not find

them. He was a Secret Service Agent and in a war. Gone too much at nights—doctoring and on Pinkerton assignments. Wasn't she justified in deserting? Immature and demanding, this Elizabeth, and neglectful beyond endurance, he argued.

Three hundred dollars for alimony. Jerry, Charles, and Loretta must be awarded to the mother—a heavy blow. Daniel wept, then brushed his tears aside with a deep bitterness and swore he would wipe this segment of his life away forever. He would not look back. Salve the wound with obliteration.

He returned to Richmond to secure information on the Reb defenses. An abolitionist never quits.

Hurry. No time to waste. Get this report back to the Union. Secret? Hell yes! The stealth of the Indian, the candor of the fool, and watch out, always leery, careful, expectant, like a steel wire drawn from the Gulf to Canada. Better than six foot of steel nerves, caution, and experience. Your goddamned right, experience. No damn place for a suckin' green horn.

My boys helped me beat the hell outta Col. Chiles. Wounded the hairy bastard too. Didn't expect a guerilla force. Took him by surprise. Looks damn good in a Union prison, he does.

Just missed that Missouri bushwhacker, Elkins. Got his men and all his horses though. He'll call himself Senator Stephen B. someday, the bushwhackin' bastard, like there never was a war. But we stripped him down and watched the goddamned rabbit run, and hollered, "Get some of that Mi-zoor-i poison ivy for a fig leaf." Jeez-us we laughed. Imagine takin' a bath in a war. Damned if we didn't laugh.

Back to the post and all those letters from the lady in LeClaire. Scarcely time to read them. No time to answer.

The Sioux, the Sioux. Get your duds on and join the expedition at daybreak.

It was a sight. That Knight of the plains, Spotted Tail. Trails of blood. Never get lost in this country from east to west and north to south. Follow the bloody trail. Never get lost. Yet the country's lost and mad.

King Fisher set fire to the prairie and yelped, "Indian." Burned the hell outta grub stakers. Glad my homestead wasn't windward. When they put the prairie fire out, they shouted in Bee-AT-rice, "King Fisher's mad, King Fisher's mad. Burn him in his own fire." They shouted this in Bee-AT-rice territory of Nebraska.

Westward of Beatrice, to mop up the debris of the massacre. Bury the dead, house the living, console the fear-stricken survivors. Old man Eubanks dazed in his doorway pointing his Winchester heavenward. Behind him his wife and all four younguns—scalped. That was the massacre of '64. Then the depredation claims. House burned, wagons burned, food stolen. It could all be replaced with a claim, Joe Roper. But little Laura? No claim will bring a stolen girl back. But Dan made out the claim just the same and filed it.

But it was our fault. Pushed from the Atlantic onto the plains, from the plains to beyond, and from there? A man can only take so much pushin', white man, red, black man. Only so much pushin'.

A short leave for Dan gave him time to tell Agnes the war's end was near. It gave him the courage to speak to her of coming West and sharing the cabin on Cub Creek. And it gave her time to accept. There followed many letters to this quiet lady in LeClaire of the flowing future they could have together.

The end of 1864 found Daniel hurrying to his squatter's cabin. He readied it for the lady. The dilapidated log stable was reinforced and cleaned for his team's arrival later.

As was the custom, they were married in the home of John and Eliza Wright Suiter, Agnes' parents. This union took place on the eighth day of February, 1865. They lingered only shortly visiting the Suiter family before leaving for an equally short visit to Daniel's parents in Abingdon. Agnes, the only daughter in a family of five males, would be sorely missed.

At the kitchen door of his tiny frame home, John Suiter called his daughter to him for the last time before she left. He took from his pocket a thousand dollar check and asked his daughter to pin it inside her corset in his presence. "You are only twenty two, Aggie, and Daniel thirty nine. You are young. If you ever need to use it to get home, do so. If you don't need it for that purpose, you'll have it for another." The money secured, they embraced, and Agnes fled tearfully to the rented spring wagon and Daniel, waiting in the seat, lines in hand.

She did not mind the long trek to Nebraska with Daniel. She was used to the rugged life of her riverboat pilot father on the Mississippi. She was well prepared. What she was not ready to accept was parting from her family. Her adjustment was to come slowly and with difficulty. She endured, for wherever Daniel led, she would follow.

From Abingdon they traveled to Eddyville, Iowa where Dan had left his team of black Indian ponies and his spring wagon. The young bride's oak hope chest was carefully loaded onto the wagon. The chest, built by her father, and the few linens and finery it contained were her most valued possessions. Dan brought mainly books. The most important, *Scudder and Scudder*, the texts he'd used in medical school, were wrapped in oil skin and carefully placed in the wagon box. He had become more of a frontiersman than a doctor during the war and he preferred this, but he would have need for the books.

The trip was long and cold. Fortunately the winter was relatively mild. The horses, Gyp and Julie, tripped along steadily. Agnes found it was a good time to better know this big man who sat so erect beside her, who was both

fierce and gentle, unconcerned and kind. Dan also used the
time to know his young lady better—to be able to add
"grand" to the title of lady he'd given her. A grand lady,
intelligent, stable, and compassionate. She was the kind of
foundation this often fierce looking man needed.

At Rockport, Missouri the ferry was frozen in the river.
There was a half day's delay while six men worked to chop
it free and chop a path through to the open channel.
Daniel, eager to help, wielded a long pole and shoved the
broken chunks of ice into the current while the other men
clubbed and swung axes against the frozen bond.

In early March, Daniel related the history of the Beatrice
settlement to Agnes as they jogged toward the prairie
village.

"In 1857 three hundred people on the steamer Hannibal
headed up river for Nebraska City. There were a number of
Mormons aboard who carried on their religious devotions
on board as they would anywhere." Dan was in fine fettle
doing the thing he most enjoyed, telling a story. "The story
goes that, in spite of the fact there were more Mormons
than non-Mormons, the non-Mormons gathered and set
forth an edict."

Agnes couldn't help giggling and her long brown curls
bounced from the edges of her bonnet like coil springs in
rhythm with the wagon.

"This is a fact, Agnes." Dan was slightly dismayed at her
giggling. "It damn truly did happen."

Agnes pursed her lips and sobered for the sake of the
story, secretly enjoying Dan's consternation.

"Well, damnit, they thanked God, that though inferior in
numbers, there were enough honest, honorable, pure, and
noble men and women to redeem that otherwise ill fated
cargo of human lives. They said there was enough germs of
human and divine principle to counteract that evil influence
so they could establish in this new country pure civiliza-
tions. Something they could damn well point to with pride

that would be full of love and honor and they'd be
high-minded Americans by divine right." He slapped his
thigh mightily and laughed heartily. Gyp and Julie's ears
flicked back and forth at the raucous laughter.

Agnes suppressed a grin.

"After that damned high and mighty soundin' stuff, they
went through a whole fal-de-ral about the sharp-witted
lawyer that was comin' out here to practice his honored
profession and who was gonna weigh justice for his bread
and make a goddamned fortune from the squabbles of his
neighbors. This was to teach lawbreakers a lesson. A
Goddamn shyster come out to bleed the hell outta some
poor devil, all to teach him a lesson. Some lesson! Teach
the halfwits never to go back to the damn crooked lawyer,
that's what it'd teach 'em."

Agnes was enjoying it all. Her Daniel was a pleasant
entertainer.

"There was a doctor on board too. Come to heal
everybody with patent medicines and physic. By the time
this damned doctor and the laywers finished, there'd be a
few desperate souls and a whole slew of goddamned coon
hounds left for the speculators to pick to the bones. They
said the speculators could do little harm and doubtless
much good. The coon hounds could probably hold their
own, but the damned humans lost their britches." They
laughed merrily together.

"And Beatrice. Did they name the town after Dante's
muse? I think that rather poetic."

"Hell no. They named it after some old maid or the
hungriest coon hound in the pack. One or the other."

Agnes laughed but asked no more. The mood had
changed and shown in his answer. She would leave him to
his thoughts while she observed more of the endless prairie
passing by her.

Gyp and Julie were skillful in avoiding prairie dog
mounds. Occasionally they drew the wagon over a mound

and the inevitable impact when it dropped was shattering.

The white frothy clouds rolled over each other allowing
short glimpses of the deep pure blue sky. The crisp air,
pure and clean and invigorating to the team, was chilling to
the riders. They dismounted periodically and walked briskly
beside the team to warm up. The land was beautiful with
its rising swells and twisting draws. The ground had thawed
enough on this late winter day to let a track slice through
the heavy dry grass. South sides of slopes, bare of grass,
succumbed to the heavy wagon and let it sink to the axle.
Dan avoided the spots protected by the sun where he could
to spare the team. The woolly buffalo grass hugged the
slopes with its thick dry shag. "It's dormant now," Dan
said. "But it's beautiful and soft when it's green."

They had passed few trees since the bluff of the
Missouri. In the distance the gray trees, stripped of their
foliage for winter, formed a winding design across the dull
amber countryside. A few log huts huddled on a swell.
"That's Beatrice," Dan announced.

Agnes' heart sunk. Nine or ten log cabins and a log store.
She drew in her breath, sat more erect, and pressed her lips
tightly together. If this were not enough to discourage a
travel weary lady from the East, the next announcement
should have been.

"Another stream to cross. This time a big one. You'll
have to cross on the skiff, Agnes. We're at the banks of the
Big Blue River. We're only four miles from home."

The narrow skiff was returning from the opposite bank
of the river, swollen from pre-spring thaws. The skiff
operator Mr. Cartwright, had just deposited a woman and
boy on the other side where they waited for the man on
horseback to lead a brindle milk cow across on a rope
behind him. The cow got mid-stream, became frightened of
the swirling water, and refused to budge. She began to bawl
and paw the water. The man drew the rope taut against his
saddle horn urging the horse on. The horse struggled against

the rope tied to the immobile cow, then began to flounder
and frighten himself. The cow squatted on her rear in the
water and bawled piteously while the water washed over
her head. Her front feet flailed violently, catching in the
ropes and causing her to roll wildly down stream. The
horse lost ground and was being pulled downstream by the
cow. The woman and child on the bank screamed frantically and uncontrollably. "Shoot the poor beast. My God
shoot her," she screamed. "Don't let her suffer no more."
She waved her arms frantically, then rolled her apron across
her face tightly. "Shoot the poor creature, Henry. Dear
God, don't let her suffer no more." Her scream rolled into
a weeping wail not unlike the bawl from the soaked cow.

Agnes clung to the skiff with her oak chest beside her as
Mr. Cartwright steered a wide arc around the flailing cow.
She could almost sympathize with the wailing woman on
the bank when she saw the cow's eyes drawn back into her
head so that only the whites showed. By the time Mr.
Cartwright deposited her chest safely on the bank, Dan had
unhitched his team and was riding Gyp out to the cow.
While Henry positioned his horse for another pull, Dan
found the animal's tail and pulled her to her feet. Prodded
from both ends, the cow followed the line of least resistance and let the horse lead her onto the bank no worse
for the ordeal. Agnes went to the hysterical woman who
was calming down now that the cow was out of the water.
If she would lose her head over this, what would she do in
a real emergency? The Henry she had called upon to shoot
the cow was soaked and shivering. The boy had wet himself
during the excitement and stood, thin and pale, shivering.
The woman, more interested in social amenities then
comfort, introduced her husband, Henry Odell. Agnes
nodded, but she wished the fool woman would take care of
the wetted child.

Dan finished placing the logs beneath his covered wagon
at the water's edge. Gyp and Julie stood patiently in the

icey water waiting for their order to cross. The logs would
help buoy the heavy wagon in the deep water so it would
at least partially float. "Gyp, Julie," Dan clucked, and
braced himself in a standing position in the front of the
wagon box. The team moved slowly feeling for footing.
The wagon was heavy against the resistance of the logs
beneath it. The swirls in the middle, those were the
dangerous ones. If they could get through that . . . . Dan
was an expert horseman. A gentle man with animals. Gyp
and Julie hit the boiling pockets first. No footing to feel
for here. They must swim. The harness floated loose above
their backs as they swam skillfully, drawing the floating
wagon and logs behind them. The current caught the wagon
broadside and started turning it, pulling the team back-
wards downstream. The horses fought desperately to hold
their load and make headway. They were losing ground—
forty feet of it—a hundred feet of it. Dan remained calm,
speaking gently to his team.

Agnes followed the riverbank downstream watching her
Daniel fighting the angry water. The wagon turned again,
the horses were caught sideways in front of it. It would tip
and Daniel would be killed. Before she ever saw her new
home she would be a widow. But the experienced team
righted themselves and thrust ahead pulling the load from
the heavy current. Up the steep bank and the job was
done.

The deep ruts in the trail to their homestead were frozen
now in the dusk of this March thirteenth. Darkness fell
before they reached the ravine that separated Joe Graff's
rough hewn log cabin from Dan's. Graff came out with a
lighted lantern to help the Freemans across the ravine.

Home at last. Dan lit an oil lamp that cast a pale yellow
light across the dirt floor of the single room. Agnes waited
for him, not so much to light a fire in the crude fireplace
but to gather her own senses and the wonder of this, her
new home. It was soon warm and, despite the crude

interior, cozy in comparison to the dark chill outside. The cabin had a half window on the south side. There were two oak benches and the straight hard chair Daniel brought from the wagon. The bed was built into the wall and the mattress was filled with hay.

The next morning Nathan Blakely returned the four lid, wood-burning cook stove which would bake the first biscuits and fry the first grouse made by the lady whom everyone said Dan was sure to bring to this prairie.

# III

# Loneliness of a Lady

### 1866 — 1870

In daylight the loneliness of the homestead was not quite so awesome to Agnes. Dan took her to the crest of the hill overlooking his claim along Cub Creek. "It's this spot that decided me on it," he told her. "I'll build a bigger house off to the north and at a higher water level. Down there I'll make the stable. Soon's the ground is ready, I'll break more sod and get some corn in." His dark eyes sparkled with enthusiasm.

"I like the big oak trees. They seem to stand guard over the cabin, Daniel. I like them."

"You afraid?"

"No. Not unless those pesky Indians bother. Are they apt to?"

"Apt to. Don't get scared, though. The reservation is just south of here. Likely any that come will only be Otoe, or maybe some Missouri. They won't hurt you."

"How will I know if they're Otoe or Sioux?"

"You won't. But don't go a worryin' anyway. I'm gonna ride Julie into town for some supplies. Keep inside the house, I won't be gone long. Indians do come, give them what they want. But, damnit, don't go gettin' scared."

She wouldn't. She was already that way. She hoped Daniel didn't notice.

Dusk came and Daniel was not home. She had busied herself with putting the few things she had away and making the drab room homier. The corn bread was baked and the beans simmered. She waited for Daniel's return, wondering if he was always late.

When Dan walked in, there was a merry twinkle in his

eyes. He carried a sad-faced hound under his arm and handed
it to Agnes. She set it on the floor promptly. It was neither
proper nor sanitary to hold a dog.

"I got that dog for your protection, Aggie. A man has
no damn business living on the prairie without a dog."

She could not imagine the dog protecting anything as she
watched it cower on the floor. "He's just a little coward,
Daniel. No good for anything." She was angry that Dan
had offered no explanation for his tardiness.

"Goddamnit-to-hell, she's a fine dog and she'll whelp a
sassy batch of pups. I had to go all the way to Blue Springs
to find her. She's one hell of a fine dog." He knelt to rub
her ears as he spoke.

"I suppose if you think we ought to keep her, she's a
fine dog, but not in the house." She could see Daniel
wanted the animal and, though she wanted no part of the
dog, she decided it was best to let him have his way.

"Dammit-to-hell, Aggie, you aren't back East now. The
dog stays in the house till she's used to things."

The dog stayed.

The old St. Deroin freight road ran through the homestead on one side to the north. It met with the Oregon trail
north of Fairbury and originated at Brownville, later the
route started from Nebraska City. The end of March saw
the beginning of covered wagon migration westward
through the homestead. As the early spring wore on, the
flow increased. Cub Creek was the spot for pure clean
spring water perpetually oozing from its west bank ahead
of the cabin. If nightfall caught travelers near the creek,
Dan made them welcome to camp and use the plentiful
wood supply along the banks.

Canvas-covered wagons crawled along the rutted trail
pulled by Missouri and Illinois oxen or a pair of jackrabbit-
eared mules or slow horses. Agnes was grateful for the
visual company the passing travelers afforded as they drove
by. Dan often walked over to the spring where they

stopped for water and got acquainted.

"Hamilton? My name's Freeman," he'd say. "After a homestead?"

"The woman's got relations out by Fort Kearney. Kinda thought we'd see what she's like out there. Been on the road since the 28th day of February."

"Southern Iowa, hunh. My missus is from LeClaire."

"Did she know the Caldwells in LeClaire? They's my Ma's people." The woman was anxious. The women were always anxious and fretful in their attempt to cover up their homesickness.

"Damned if I know. Never heard her mention them."

"Don't wanta sell your dog? We lost ours back along the Missouri. Sure miss the little cuss." Hamilton scooped the black and tan into his arms and played with her ears.

"Oh, hell, I couldn't sell Tanny. The missus couldn't part with her." Dan reached for the dog his missus wouldn't touch.

"That right? My woman don't like dogs none, but travelin' this way a man oughta have one." He eyed Tanny once more wishfully.

"My missus is right set on this one—but you're right, no man ought to be without a dog. Most damn humans don't know how to act without a dog to tell them how." The men exploded with such laughter it frightened Tanny from Dan's arms. She yelped twice and ran for the cover of the Freeman wagon sitting in the yard beside the house, her tail between her legs.

"She's just a pup yet," Dan said in way of defending the long eared hound's behavior. He loved dogs of any kind, any number or nature.

So it went with most of the wagons that crossed his homestead. Dan was congenial, helpful, and generous to a fault with the weary people who rode them. If they needed firewood to cook their supper, he waved the whole timber of Cub Creek to them and a camping spot to boot, so long as they didn't molest the wildlife. If they were hungry, he'd invite them to the house and ask Agnes to feed them white biscuits and molasses, even though they often had barely enough for themselves. If they were sick, he doctored them, gave them medicine and let them stay on.

Agnes liked doctoring. She studied from Dan, pored over his medical books, and later subscribed to a medical journal. Years later, when Nebraska passed a licensing law for the practice of medicine, she took the examination and became a licensed physician. She didn't practice long after that because of her advancing age.

It wasn't long before Dan began keeping a guest book of signatures from every person passing along the trail. He was always hopeful that somehow a relative of his or Agnes might be among the emigrating flocks that passed.

Late in 1864, while Dan was readying his cabin for his bride, he was elected coroner. Knowing he would soon be living on the homestead, the community was anxious to have his medical experience in such an office. He had practiced for eleven years in Illinois, but the war and the sad experience of his first marriage tended to divert his interest from medicine. He used his training during the war as a practical disguise for a secret service agent. He could easily penetrate enemy lines posing as a doctor and gain much needed information for the Union. His desire for a medical career had been stifled by a too persistent woman. He could not heal his own wound and gradually lost interest in healing others. The land was his tonic and when that became dilute, the restlessness, searching, seeking would emerge.

Cash was scarce. Until a crop could be grown it would become scarcer. The sod must be broken, the seeds dropped. Spring came early in '65. The sod plow sliced through the roots of the heavy grasses and chunks of fresh black soil curled around the moulboard and dropped over, burying the grass. The insects housed among the buried

roots scurried from their hiding and faced a bright April
sun. In boots curled at the toes from many soakings and
worn to the raw red leather, Dan tramped behind in the
narrow furrow. Spring bugs flitted past the mare's ears. The
plow lay sliced through the slender damp roots. The
meadowlarks strutted across the fresh plowed earth and
filled upon the scurrying insects and the occasional sluggish
white grubs.

Dan leaned back to hold the tied lines taut around his
waist, his thick arms guiding the balky twisting handles.

"Hya, hya. Geed-up. 'M on Jul' 'm on." He prodded the
horse to pull her load. Every round he'd stop and pull the
plow out of the ground and file the lay sharper. It was
brutal work for both the horse and man. A half day's work
gnawing through the tangle of grass roots would blunt the
lay and make it necessary to pound it flat again. A couple
of days plowing and the share would have to be taken to
town again for Jake Shaw to draw out in his sooty
blacksmith shop.

Once the clearing was plowed, Agnes was less appre-
hensive about her surroundings. She could look out across
twenty or thiry acres of open ground and see what might
be coming, and she grew more dependent upon Tanny's
alert bay as the dog grew older, so she fell to her work
more peacefully.

After an early morning prairie schooner with a spotted
cow trailing behind rumbled off the homestead, Dan hurried to the house to announce the news the travelers
brought. "Abraham Lincoln has been assassinated!" The
fire sprang into his deep eyes once again and he sat down
amidst a flurry of oaths. Agnes was less startled by the
news than by the dark look behind his wild beard. He was
probably remembering the time he first met Lincoln, back
in Illinois when they were both hunting ducks along the
Sangamon River. He'd never been a Republican. He'd
favored his father's whig ideals and added his own

abolitionist fervor to his thinking until he met and talked
to Lincoln. After their meeting, he rode to every speech
and debate he could get to that this lanky man participated
in. It was never the party he followed, only the man. Now
the man was dead. Dan sat immobile for some time, Agnes
neither daring nor caring to disturb him. He didn't like the
way the Republican party had handled the South. Too
damned autocratic and too cruelly. Sure, he was an abolitionist and a Northerner, but he was human too. Why the
hell kick a man once he's down? There would be no reason
to follow the party any longer without the man whom he
felt made that party. His feet shuffled and a low growl
crawled from his throat. He stood, "I am no longer a
Republican." With this announcement he turned abruptly
and strode from the house without another word.

Agnes knew his hurt. She would not interfere. Shortly,
his wagon rumbled by the house toward Beatrice. He went
to engage in the discussions sure to be going on in
Townsend's. He would make a few ripples of his own to
dispel his gloom.

The ways of the frontier were tough and often callous.
They were motivated by expediency and desperate need.
Currency was only a word between crops. Sickness was a
weak opiate for deprivation and hunger, and the men with
any guts and salt planted their woman in their soddy or
cabin and took off looking for work to supplement their
living. If the women had the brains for survival and the
courage to make out and get ahead, they stayed where
their men planted them, reared their families amidst the
chickens, cows, and hogs his money provided, and
weathered the bad times with the good. Any who varied
from this pattern, except for a handful of people tossed
across the whole frontier who were lucky enough to come
to this country with money, would have starved the first
six months. Men who didn't leave home to work and who
tried to make their living solely from the soil in the

beginning, oftentimes found their names heading a homestead abandonment claim in the local newspaper. They
turned back East, worse off than when they came.

Dan Freeman doctored between crops, setting his home
up as an office. "Doc", they called him in town—"Doc
Freeman." When doctoring was scarce at home, he packed
the covered wagon with straw for a bed, hitched the black
Indian ponies to it, and went south, southeast, or southwest. He'd be gone a month or six weeks, always returning
with a herd of cattle or horses he'd received for pay, and
usually with a new dog or two in the wagon seat beside
him. Once he came home with a pack of worthless burrows
to show for his effort. What could he do with them? This
enterprising man would have an answer. "Jerky," he said,
"what the hell else." At least they were worth a joke.
Agnes knew he didn't have the heart to get rid of them.
Finally, when his precious stack of hay dwindled and the
last forkful mired into manure under the tramping hooves,
Dan took them out on free range and let them loose. He
corralled the cattle and horses he'd received in pay along
the creek. He often had as many as a hundred cattle and a
hundred horses at a time. When they'd fattened some, he
sold them and bought land—abandoned homesteads and
town lots. Agnes dutifully kept the home place going while
her Daniel was away. Her only objection to her role was
the ungovernable loneliness she had felt since the day she
left her parent's doorstep. She hated everything about the
prairie and the rough cabin she lived in. She often fled to
the corn patch and flung herself behind a shock so Daniel
wouldn't see her from the house and wept her loneliness
dry. The only thing that kept her on the prairie was her
sense of duty and her awesome admiration for that huge
man, sometimes fiery sometimes pouting, but always gentle
with her.

One of the final attempts made by the Cheyenne in the
Gage County area was their entry into the west edge of the

Otoe reservation where they intimidated the Otoe into
turning over their live stock. On their foray into and out of
the area they molested homesteaders in soddies west and
north of the Little Blue River. They scattered cattle as far
as the Platte River, and looted and burned what was left. A
group of several men from around Beatrice took arms and
rode west to run the Cheyenne back onto the reservation.
Dan Freeman and Horace Wickham rode towards Dewitt
and picked up Abel Cox who had just had a skirmish with
a small group of Cheyenne along the creek behind his
house. They helped Cox bury the seven dead Cheyenne he
had picked off with his Spencer Army rifle, before riding
westward to join the government troops who were out
trying to round up the Cheyenne. The incident proved to
be more scare than problem and the Beatrice group returned home. The three men continued on towards the
Platte, rounded up the homesteaders' cattle and brought
them back to Dan's homestead. Dan rode into Beatrice and
found the sheriff. "You're the sheriff, Chandler, I've got
seventy nine head of milling bawling cattle corralled on my
place with appetites like you never saw. Notify those
people to come get the goddamned things."

Chandler was curt and indifferent. "How the hell you
'spect me to notify 'em? I don't know who all's got cattle
missin'."

"I found the cattle, damnit-to-hell, you find the people.
If you ain't got sense enough for that, then get the hell out
of your job." He whirled and stalked to his horse, angry at
a man who wouldn't help another. Chandler found the
owners slowly, but not before the cattle had eaten most of
Dan's feed. The cattle owners were grateful and paid for
the feed their stock had eaten, but Dan retained a deep
dislike for Chandler over the encounter. When he disliked a
man, it was intense and permanent.

The first crop the Freemans put in was 20 acres of corn.
The ground prepared, Agnes followed Dan as he lightly

jabbed a pointed stick into the earth. With the bag of seed
thrown across his broad shoulders, he dropped a kernel into
each hole, then stepped on it to cover it. Twenty acres of
jabs and kernel dropping, but it was done. It was a good
growing season. The rains came right and the soil fed the
plants well. It gave Dan time to cut and peel the logs for
the new house he'd promised Agnes. It would take a whole
season of cutting to have enough. But Agnes' interest was
not in the logs that were to go into the house. Her
thoughts were in Iowa. Dan watched her with troubled
eyes. He recognized the homesickness that gnawed at her.
"Aggie, I'll be gone for a spell." He laid his ax aside,
bridled Gyp, and headed towards Hoag. He met Wib Rogers
in the yard. "There'll be a meeting at our house tomorrow
evening to organize a neighborhood lyceum. Tell Blakeleys
and Coffins, and Riddles and, damnit, bring the women
folks."

The first meeting went well with visiting and planning
and getting acquainted with the neighbors. "You a college
graduate? My, we have a school teacher, Dave, right here.
We got two boys needs schoolin'." Before the evening was
done, Agnes had agreed to teach seven boys in her home
that fall, the first school in Blakely township. Her pay was
the seventeen dollar aggregate the parents could spare. It
helped to keep her mind from straying to Iowa and from
worrying about bringing their young one into such a wild
world.

Dan delivered their first child January 27, in 1866. They
named her Eliza and her father dubbed her Dade. Agnes
gave her full attention to this new child. She would help
dispel the loneliness of the prairie forever for her tender
mother. If the grasses were foreboding stockades of fear
before, they suddenly became a haunting nightmare of
worry to the new mother. Every motion of the grasses a
possible Indian, every snake a looming threat. When the
child began to toddle, the tall forest of grasses became like

threatening jaws, ready to swallow up the infant forever.

Tanny's early litter of pups crawled everywhere this spring when brother John Suiter came to visit his sister and the new Eliza. Just twenty one, he was eligible to file claim on a homestead. He liked Dan and Agnes and he liked the land next to theirs. It seemed natural to file claim on the 160 to the north of Dan's. "You need a cabin, I need a new one. We'll build them where the claims divide with just enough room between to satisfy the skeptics," Dan said. Brother John could help whittle a few logs, but he couldn't stay to build his cabin. "Sure, I'll do it," Dan offered, But first he must get trees planted—the right kind.

A wagon trip to Peru where a fresh stock of nursery trees had recently been shipped gave Dan enough peach trees to plant a half mile line of them, three rows deep, from his favorite look-out point on the east hill straight down to Cub Creek. Parallel to these he planted his favorite shade tree, the lofty cottonwood, down the slope and to the creek. He sunk roots to half as many apple trees as he did peach and several hundred pear and plum trees this same year. His bent for agriculture was mainly for fruit trees. He lost himself much of his life in splicing, grafting, and working with his huge fruit orchard. A secondary product of his horticultural enterprises which gave him as much pleasure as the fruit trees was the wildlife and birds the bearing trees attracted.

Agnes and little Eliza spent much time with him when he planted the trees. Agnes was too frightened to stay in the cabin for long, and she enjoyed watching him work with the pruning knife and splicing the grafts.

If there was bread to bake and she could not get out, she found herself casting furtive glances to the window and keeping Eliza's whereabouts in the room well fixed in her mind. On one occasion she looked up to see a face framed by the window peering in at her. Only the child on the floor made her move to the door and bolt it. The face still

peered. "If they know you are there, you must give them
what they want, or else there's trouble." Dan had told her.
She was seen, but did she have the courage to unbolt the
door and let them in? She snatched up Eliza and slowly
undid the door latch. The shadow from the window
disappeared and became life size in front of the doorway.
There were two. She had to suppose they were friendly.
They came into the house. "Pony corn," one spoke. "Pony
corn," and began going through her pans and oven.
Knowing he would take the fresh corn bread anyway, she
forced herself to appear the benefactor and offered it to
them. She clutched the baby tightly, supposing they would
take the cornbread and disappear. Instead, they squatted in
the center of the floor and ate the food. The stench of the
loin skin skunk hide on one was overpowering. When they
finished eating, they investigated a few more pans and
finding nothing they wanted, padded out the door. The
door was left open the remainder of the day in a futile
attempt to get rid of the skunk odor. It was her first
experience with the friendly Otoe. Though Dan got along
well with them and there was mutual respect between
them, she was fearful for as long as they remained on the
reservation to the south of the Freeman homestead, even
though she learned if they didn't get what they wanted
they'd simply come back another time. She became more
accustomed to them the more they came, but she could
never completely feel at ease.

There was talk again of Cheyenne who had fled the
reservation and who were working their way toward the
Missouri River, this time to take the herds of the peaceful
Otoe and everything else in their way. Dan remained close
to his cabin for days and crept into the woods at night to
watch his house. "I can be a hell of a lot more help to my
home and family if I'm outside than in," he'd say. Agnes
understood the logic of his argument, but her instincts
needed him inside with her.

As soon as the Cheyenne scare subsided, a half dozen
Otoe drew panic when they went into Steven's Creek north
of Beatrice and stole some clothing. Dan had to leave for
his second load of saplings at Peru and was disturbed to
leave his family during the height of the emotional up-
heaval. To assure his family's safety and to calm Agnes, he
rode to the Indian reservation and sought out Chief
Arkeketa. "I must go to the big wicked city," he explained,
"and I am afraid someone will steal my gold watch.
Therefore I give it to you for safekeeping until I return so
nothing will happen to it or to my family who remain at
home." He handed his gold watch with chain over to
Arkeketa and they shook hands. He knew that if he put
the Chief in a position of trust, he would not break his
word. This assured him that no harm would come to his
family while he was away.

Agnes was not so reassured as her husband, but since
Dan's trip was inevitable and since she must sometime learn
to accept the ways of the new wild land, she accepted her
fate. True to Arkeketa's word, no harm ever came to Agnes
on the homestead. But after the bond of trust had been
cemented between the Chief and the booming homesteader,
Agnes found herself dishing up molasses and cornbread
more frequently to a silent and steady trickle of visitors
from the reservation. This pleased the congenial Daniel.
"Those damned missionaries have tried to convert these
people since they found them here," he told Agnes one
evening as they rested under one of the big oaks. "Come
out here to adapt the Indian's low level of culture to
theirs," he mimicked the words in contempt as he said
them. "The children went around nude and they believed
in Waconda, not God, and damned if it didn't hurt those
church people." He laughed loudly at his own comment.

Agnes smiled. "It is ridiculous, isn't it? I wonder how
they'd feel if the situation was reversed?"

"It's damned downright wrong. That's what it is," he

rubbed his chin through the tangled beard. "But they never look at it from anybody else's viewpoint, cause they haven't got sense enough to. Too damned much probin' into others business, that's what. Who the hell's that comin over the bridge? Nathan Blakely? Come sit, come sit," he boomed as the man came nearer.

"Thought I'd come sit a spell," Nathan explained as he squatted on a block of wood.

"Gonna have a good corn crop, Dan?"

"Hell yes." He answered, not so much convinced of the crop as he was exuberant with the words.

"Gonna break more sod this fall?"

"No. I have to build a bigger house. Mebbe I can do both."

Nathan fidgeted for a time before he could get the courage to ask, "Mrs. Freeman, you 'spose you could spare some 'lasses? I'm clean out an' I can't stand to eat no flapjacks without 'lasses."

Agnes gave Eliza to her father and went to the house for the "'lasses."

A crop had been harvested and twenty more acres of prairie grass broken, ready to seed. Logs were cut, peeled, and ready for the house. March 1, 1867, Nebraska became the 37th state. The government had given alternate sections of land to the railroad to spur rail development across the country. Panicky businessmen in Beatrice tried to woo the rails in their direction, fearful lest some brash, foolhardy soul would anger the rapidly growing dinosaurs of monopoly and their fair city would be deprived of a railroad. Little did they realize that this mammoth concern whose thrust was a gift of the American government would never stop until it threaded its way to every hamlet in the nation. But panic grows deep with frightened souls and bickering soon ensues. A man who condemned the massive railroads was looked upon as a man who would thwart the small towns—cut his own brother's throat.

"The rails are no respector of man," Dan said. "They're a cruel and cold monopoly that sweeps through the choicest soil on a man's homestead and says it belongs to them. The little man? To hell with the little man. They don't give a damn for him."

Who's this Dan Freeman to question the massive railroad? Burn him, burn him, we want our railroads.

"The railroad is too big, too powerful. The man becomes its slave," Dan plead, "A rail line, yes, but don't destroy the little man."

In twenty years, our town will become a city of 50,000 people if we have our rails. Give us our rails and iron horse.

By fall, Dan with the help of Sam Nedrow and John Kelly had built two cabins. One on the Freeman homestead, the other across the dividing line for brother John Suiter's new claim. Clapboards were latched to the roof for shingles and covered with slabs of sod.

"Tight as the end of a woodpile," John Kelly said satisfied.

"Fit for a Queen," Sam Nedrow claimed. But the queen who was to occupy the new log house was not interested in its size or construction. Thoughts of Iowa and the squirming within her occupied her thoughts. On the 18th day of December, 1867, in a new state and in a new cabin, baby Samuel was born.

The children added a new dimension to Agnes' life. Where before she clung to dreams and hopes of her LeClaire in Iowa, now she immersed her loneliness in her children. They were her life to be sheltered, cared for, protected, and loved—loved fiercely and precariously.

In the fall of '69, on September 1st, the patent for this grant of land Homestead entry no. 1, proof 1, page 1, volume 1 of the homestead records in the U.S. land office, Washington, D. C. was issued and signed by Ulysses S. Grant, President of the United States of America. On January 1870 the Deed Record "F" page 114, was inscribed in the record books in the office of county clerk, Beatrice, Nebraska.

"Dan'l, we need a good sheriff in Gage County. Whyn't you run for the office? Wash Rogers watched the whiskers move over the twitching of Dan's jaws.

"Yeah." John Kelly absently swept a path clean by his boot with the dead branch he toyed with. "You know what the hell your doin' an that fella in there's a sassy bird."

"Don't nobody like sass." Wash stretched himself on the stack of logs. "Not nobody." He watched Dan carefully.

Finally, Dan answered, "I ain't hankerin' for a damn job like that. Ever body'll want ya to wash their backside proper an' overlook all the damn dirt they pull." He continued to run his thumb slowly across the sharp edge of the ax thoughtfully, feeling it.

"That's the kind a sheriff there orta be. One what don't give no damn 'bout whether some high n' mighty bastard likes it or don't." Sam Nedrow spat the brownish gob, aiming for the dried sunflower six feet in front of him. The slime caught in the top and dripped to the ground in a syrupy stringy ooze. He watched his aim carefully, followed each drop as it slid to the ground. He shifted the cud in his mouth to the other cheek, carefully settled it, and turned back to Dan. "Make a leetle currency too. That never hurt no man."

"Wish you'd swallow that goddamn battle ax. I'd sooner you'd yank yer britches down and aim at my damn sunflowers." He thought of the exchange between him and the sheriff over the homesteader's cattle. He was a smart alec all right. Ought to give him a little scare by puttin' my name against his. "I might just do that." He began to enjoy the idea of watching this man he couldn't like squirm a bit. Just for a lesson, of course. He laughed vociferously.

The lesson turned out to be one in reverse and Dan was stuck with the job of sheriff for the next three years. This meant a move to Beatrice with his family and hiring Dave Byers to tend the cabin, homestead, and the homestead stock.

"I don't mind being in town away from the worry of the Indians," Agnes exclaimed, "but to uproot ourselves over such a foolish thing." She wondered if she would ever get used to this impetuous man.

The stay in Beatrice did give Agnes respite from the Indians and a chance to neighbor more and forget about Iowa. It also gave her a new son, James, born February 27, 1870.

The rounds of duty drew Doc Dan into conversations with the attorneys in town and into the ways of their litigations. It was a new avenue not yet explored by this frontier knowledge seeker who had the compulsion to know the whys and wherefors of every crevice of man's existence. Once he found an answer, satisfaction still eluded him. There must be more, always there must be more that he did not see. The duty of the job itself soon became boring and ridden with pestering favor seekers who annoyed the man.

The men gathered at Townsend's or Pap Towle's whenever they felt like a discussion or had some news of the world to impart. Nothing delighted Dan more than a good political discussion. His interest was keen and his knowledge of politics was broad.

"I'll agree with you on religion, but I can't on politics," Cap Ashby said hotly. "You don't see things like I do."

"If I was to see things like you do, I'd in a damn hurry change my politics." Dan retorted with an animated guffaw.

"You used to be a strong Republican, you say you're for a party of the people. Well, that's exactly what the Republican party is."

"The hell you say."

"Well, what the hell's the whig party? It don't

stand for a damn." Cap was getting angry.

Dan was highly amused by this man and his mounting
anger. The uproarious laughter only served to aggravate
Ashby more until he stalked from the meeting room, his
neck red and burning. "You probably think we bought a
gold mine when we got all that snow and ice they call
Alaska, too," he shot over his shoulder.

Dan laughed all the harder. When he met Cap on the
street next day, he'd cooled off and was eager to take on
where he'd left off. Dan admired the attorney for this.

Dan and Agnes bundled the children up and watched the
dance on Washington's birthday. Dan kept a legal eye on
things while Agnes enjoyed the sights. She had never cared
much for dancing. She looked upon herself as a plain
woman and while she was always eager to help someone in
need, she was no aspirant to social stature and vigorously
disliked those who were. She much preferred the Lyceums
and Literary Societies, though she took little part in them.
Dan enjoyed the Lyceums and was eager to take part by
making a speech or more specifically by acting in the plays
they produced. He was an entertainer and enjoyed the part.
"I am content to get my fulfillment from these meetings
by watching and listening to Dan," she would say. She
shied from the limelight, but basked in her Daniel's glory.

Sometimes the Literary Society gatherings became heated
as when Cap Ashby read an essay on his philosophy of
religion and prompted Wm. Bradt to comment, "The men
have become wiser in their generation than the children of
light."

This in turn prompted Dan to spit, "And Will Bradt
hasn't got a goddamned lick of sense, so how the hell
would he know?"

# IV

# Temporary Residence

## 1871 — 1875

The East met the West in a golden union at Promontory Point. Floods of immigrants from Bohemia, Germany, Ireland and the Scandinavian countries answered the call of growing American Industry for cheap labor. The Nevada legislature provided that no Chinese should in any way be employed upon the roads, either in construction or operating capacity, when it granted charters for new roads. The article on women's suffrage was rejected from the Constitution of Nebraska. The focal point of attention was instead a heated debate over who was to be delegate to the National Convention.

Homestead abandonment notices increased in the local newspapers while a dozen wagon trains a day passed through Beatrice for Kansas and points west. The 1870 census in Beatrice counted 624 people, 96 of whom were attending school. Bay windows were in vogue, and London was nursing 20,000 cases of small pox. Beatrice sported a new courthouse and meeting place. Residents of Cub Creek were burned out by a prairie fire.

Governor Butler spoke at Tecumseh the night before a boy along the Solomon was shredded by wolves while he slept.

The B & M railroad steamed into Beatrice in December unmindful of both the critics and the wooers. It was a blooming land of new, bedmated with the savage paradoxical old, and it prompted Daniel Freeman to remark to his wife Agnes, "This country will one day soon be like the eastern seaboard, dotted with cities, corrupt as hell, and the poor damned nag will be a relic."

"Well, all you have to do is look at the change in the six years we've been here," she said. But this is good. Progress is vital." Calm and stable, Agnes' judgement was uncanny. The calmness of the woman allowed her mind to perceive the reality about her and to evaulate it unhurriedly. Under the circumstances, little escaped her and her evaluations were sound. Dan, more spirited, more artistic, found himself leaning heavily upon this stabilizing force that had recently come into his life. Dan had gotten the kind of woman he needed, and he knew it. She was an antidote for his overgenerosity, for his contempt for orthodoxy, and for his affinity for being taken advantage of by hard luck stories. She was firm in her support of his ideals and beliefs, but she was unyielding in her demand that he conform to at least some of her rather puritanical viewpoints. She was always the lady, both in her speech and dress. When she dressed up it was fashionably, when she spoke it was precise and never with more of an oath than an occasional watered-down "ah, shoot." She refused to gossip. She preferred to talk on subjects which interested usually only her or Dan, and were political or medical in nature. She and Dan carried on extensive and animated discourses on the subjects that interested them: politics, philosophy, human beings. While few people understood the machinations of the woman, fewer understood them in the man. Agnes made herself available to any call her neighbors might make for her services in treating their ills or simply sitting out a catastrophe with them.

Unyielding as her demands may have seemed, she succeeded in changing only the minor whimsies Dan exhibited. He came to her for decisions on buying and selling land or he asked for help in handling a touchy neighbor. In fact, wherever business was concerned, he relied heavily upon her judgement. He continued to swear, and with time added color to his old collection of epithets. He slipped into town occasionally without changing his shirts and squirmed into a collar only at her insistance then only when he was caught before he'd managed an escape. He was rarely home, after the children were older, except on Sundays and then only because there was nothing doing in town.

In turn, she drew his muddy boots off and rubbed his weary feet. She placated his anger with soothing sympathetic cluckings, and treated his occasional "stomping fits" with indifference until he'd spent himself on colorful and animated verbiage. Then she quietly told her Daniel, "It's time you straightened up now." With a shamed face he invariably minded.

If she spoiled him, he in turn reciprocated. She refused to do the heavy work of the home and farm. "If I raise a family," she argued, "I feel I am doing a plenty." When she said she needed a hired girl, Dan saw to it that she had one. Most of the time she had her way in rearing the children, too.

Keeping a hired girl in the house for Agnes often meant hitching Gyp and Julie to the medicine wagon and earning extra money for the luxury. It also meant extra money to pay for hired men to tend the homestead while he earned this money. If it took him from home more, Agnes endured the separation well, knowing he did it for "their comfort and to get ahead." It proved to her he was an enterprising and ambitious father.

If Dan had to be away from home practicing medicine to earn the price of a hired girl, he also endured it well. It supplanted the restlessness innate to his character and afforded him a chance to get away from Agnes when she seemed especially nagging to him. They complemented each other well. She idolized his fiery valiance and he her quiet steadfast perception. They both kept personal matters to themselves, never airing their family business publicly, much to the consternation of their neighbors and acquaintances.

Their silence on small talk and private affairs as well as Agnes' shy nature earned for them a variety of reputations from people who could little understand this. To some, "Mrs. Freeman" was thought "odd". To those who understood her, she was simply a kind and gentle woman.

Though Dan was genial and outgoing for the most part, he could frighten the bravest into running scared into hiding. His appearance and penetrating black eyes added to the fury of his fiery outbreaks against any idea he did not condone. It was not without basis that he was known as the "Moses of the plains," feared by his enemies and revered by his friends. He had been rough and unpolished as a fighter in the war and was just as tough and hard punching as a frontier homesteader. He never hesitated to let it be known how he felt on an issue.

In 1869, Colonel Cropsey of Lincoln donated block 24 of Cropsey's addition for the grounds of the first courthouse to be built in Beatrice. In addition to this donation Cropsey also gave twelve business lots adjoining the block set aside for the courthouse and one thousand dollars in cash. Contract to Binns, Phillips, and Marshall was let on the 19th day of August 1870, and the new courthouse was completed in the spring of 1871.

When Beatrice was being plotted and surveyed from public lands in 1857 to finally become conveyed to the county in 1859, the proprietors of the town reserved a block for a courthouse, bounded on the West by 8th St; the North by Ella: the East by 9th: the South by Court Street, with intention of dedicating this block to the county, but they never did convey it. It was never designated by number on the plat of the town, but was simply marked with a pair of scales. No courthouse or other building was erected on this block, therefore it remained for twelve years public land and unattached. It was simply understood to be town property. With the generous donation to the town by Cropsey, the "Courthouse Square" as it was known suddenly became available for grabs. Few people were aware of the situation Cropsey's donation placed "Court House Square" in. But the few who did know, set about to pre-empt the square by squatter's right for their personal acquisition. "A couple of Beatrice big shots, stuffed with poor man's money," were hard at work to surrepticiously claim the land before anyone was aware of their activities, and thereby add to their growing wealth.

Freeman's position as sheriff aided him in learning of this plot, but it did nothing to help him solve the problem. He came to the one source he knew could direct him best. He and Agnes discussed the matter into the night and until they were weary. It was decided that Dan would start the next morning to build a house on the block, claim it by squatter's right and, finally having legal possession of the land, turn it over to the town as a donation for a school. As Dan later proclaimed to his son Samuel, long after the incident, "There was no damned use to ask the people in town to stop the plot, they would only flock to the speculator's defense that much quicker. They cringe and comply, let every bastard with money squeeze 'em blood-less and when they're foreclosed on they turn and lick the sons-a-bitch's backsides."

The house went up rapidly with a privy alongside and a fence enclosing the whole block. Dan moved his family into the house and proceeded to take up residence.

Animosity grew heavy with the plotter whose plan had been thwarted in its embryo. He castigated Dan publicly, derided him openly, and sought to influence citizens against him at every opportunity. He went to the newspaper editors and made his sentiments known and that his power to lend or not to lend money would be felt by those who had needed financial assistance in weathering the decline of 1869 if they didn't back his maneuvers against Freeman. *The Beatrice Express* complied when it ran an unwarranted notation regarding the office of sheriff saying "Daniel, you must give way." The reasons for the yearnings and the desire to have "Daniel . . . give way" were pointedly left unsaid. The effect of such unpolitic remarks on *Express* reader's thoughts had unlimited scope and potential. The seed of doubt was planted. It would be nurtured by unwitting scapegoats, some of whom burned under the hatred of Dan's unconventional free thinking, some who through their own trickery and dishonesty had come off bested by this staunch supporter of right, and others who would simply be sucked into the mainstream of attack because of their innate lack of resistance and the need to feel they were on the popular side.

The one attribute few people ever considered in Dan when they stalked for an encounter was the valiant defense he lent to what he thought was right. If he didn't believe an issue important, he ignored it. When he did believe in an issue he fought for it, never backing down "until the highest order says I must," as he often shouted. The "Court House Square" became such an issue. If the evoked silence as to his motives on this case had been disclosed, perhaps some of the wrath might have been averted. Regardless, he chose to meet the encounter silently, boldly, and headlong. It was to become a bitter and hate-ridden encounter which would last through 14 years of court battles, cost the Moses of the plains dearly, and would, over a hundred years later, haunt the shadow of the stalwart figure when nothing but the memory of his fiery eyes remained. The tales of evil would persist, the monstrosity of the act would magnify with each succeeding generation's telling. The man and the truth would be buried.

Dan and Agnes did not feel the full wrath of their squatter action until 1874. In the meantime there were daily herds of thousands of head of Texas longhorns driven by trail toughened bosses through Gage County and Beatrice. Dan was kept busy patroling herds bedded down on public graze range west and south of town or, as often happened, the trail weary cattle sniffed out the corn in tassle or the wheat in boot of the homesteader's fenceless claims and in a few swift gulps devoured most of the crop. What remained was quickly trampled into the ground. Complaints were made and claims paid under Freeman's watchful eye before the herd moved on to railroad loading stations east of Beatrice and finally shipped into the Chicago stockyards for slaughter. When Dan wasn't chinning with trail bosses and exchanging tales with coarse-cut ramrods, he was in Townsend's or Pap Towle's laying in wait for a budding political controversy to blossom. If it were dull, he ejected a few stimulating expletives to fire it up. If he didn't like the man or what he said, he would thunder a volley of insults interspersed with epithets, concluding his attack with cutting laughter. Then he proceeded home to re-tell the episode to Agnes. "Jesus Christ I hadda laugh." His unlaughing victim had indeed learned a lesson—wariness of this big man.

Townsend's buzzed with the news. "Two men shot over by Fairbury. Goddamned Otoes."

"Who said?"

"Had to be. Happened right outside the reservation."

"You ain't sure. What the hell makes you so sure?"

"Took Whitewater prisoner, but he dodged and run like a guilty dog. Ain't that evidence enough he done the horrible heathen deed?"

"Ya, Bradt they heathens a'right. Needin' some Christian'in up, don't ya spose?" Old man Stevens watched and red line of anger spread from the sides of Bradt's nose, pleased that he'd gotten under the thin skin.

"It wouldn't hurt none. That's what's lackin' in 'em."

"Guilty dog! Religion? Who you say has got it? Jesus Christ." Cap Ashby stood up, shoved his hat over his eyes and stalked out.

"You sure ain't." Bradt shot at him, his rage spread

purplish across his face.

The men guffawed loudly at the exchange between the extremes of the two men.

When Cap sat in the indicated straight back beside the table he threw his hat on the floor beside him. "It aggravates the hell outta me when someone talks how religious he is and acts like he just crawled outta the bowels of Satan."

Dan nodded, eyes twinkling. "Preachers?"

Ashby nodded. "I don't even know why it should bother me." He wiped his forehead.

"I don't either. They don't even know what the hell religion is. Stay for supper, Agnes wants it."

Agnes turned from the stove slightly, changed her mind, turned back pushing her hair from her hot sweaty forehead and prodded the fire with unnecessary vigor with the short poker. She could spread the short rations. With a resigned sigh she drew the white biscuits from the hot oven. "Lizy, Lizy Jane. Come fetch the biscuits to the table. Sammy, get this instant out from under Tanny and wash your face and hands." Jim began to cry in the cradle. Dan and Cap were deep in conversation. Agnes' mouth drew straight and tight, her skirt swished between table and stove. Tanny eyed her warily and slunk to the security of a dark corner. Dan belly laughed and the hound drew her smooth tail to her chin. She was the only one in the room affected by Agnes' quiet wrath. Sammy kicked the table leg throughout the meal and in turn Eliza kicked Sammy's leg trying to stop him. The angrier she became the harder she kicked. The harder Sammy was kicked the more he enjoyed agitating his sister. James, with his colicy stomach, cried the mournful wail of the sufferer. The wrath evoked by Dan's generosity soon dissipated as Agnes, harried and hot, tried to cope with the clamor of her fretting children.

In the heat of the early August, Agnes bought title to her brother John's homestead. He tired of the idea of a homestead shortly after he made claim to it, but kept it until he had proved it up so he could sell it to his sister. The land would add to their comfort and aid in their financial security. Six years had passed since the quiet woman who disliked unexpected table guests but never complained had been pinned with the thousand dollar check from her father. During that time she had grown to respect her Daniel more, not less, and had only thought of returning to LeClaire at times when the loneliness overtook her. These times were growing infrequent and of shorter duration, but the check had been guarded carefully, frugally. Now they were to use it as the court drew up the transfer. The homestead would be hers side by side with Daniel's. This was like their lives—partners. A homestead for Daniel, a homestead for her. She felt independent and, consequently, equal. "No subjugation of the female as in the clannish German families," she noted with pride. "Daniel may have pouted at times and stomped in a rage, but never at me. He treated me with kindness and respect, and for that I'm eternally grateful."

"Gage County Fair? When?" Agnes was eager.

"Tenth. It's a first and everybody and his damned houn' dog is talking about it. It's aimed to be peaceful for the pleasure of the ladies and younguns. Maybe we can keep the likkered-up boys downtown in the groggeries."

Agnes laughed. "A good drubbing would do more for them. Maybe they wouldn't guzzle so much grog then." She was used to Dan's quick changes in mood.

"They'd only turn to corn cake, or Indian killin'. Hotheads are hotheads. You goin' or not, damnit?"

She would go, of course, and enjoy every minute of it.

Dan Freeman celebrated the first Nebraska Arbor day on his homestead planting hackberry and oak saplings from the banks of Cub Creek high along the north boundaries of both his and Agnes' homesteads. He set out another five hundred fruit trees, mostly cherry. On the southern

boundary of his homestead, he planted a solid row of osage
hedge that would grow into a tall sturdy tangle of thorny
brush that would excel any barb wire fence available.
Sammy followed his father from tree to hole, drawing the
freshly dug earth over the delicate roots of the saplings and
tramping the loose dirt with his small feet. For the father
the trees were a passion; for the small son, a weary endless
exhaustion. The trees would make the barren prairie a
refuge of shelter, but until they grew big enough, remnants
of the desert would still creep onto the plains and prairie as
it had in '71. A lack of rainfall dried the dying October
grasses to a brittle tinder. It had been a bad year for fires,
but the dry fall spread an explosvie blanket eager to ignite
with any courting spark: a backfire out of control, the butt
of a live coffin nail, angry lightning. Mid-October was
warmed by a raging prairie fire that swooped down from
the prairie swells, across John Scheve's farm swallowing up
94 cords of wood and on into the tall grasses and
deadwood on the west bank of Cub Creek. The flames
leapt high trying to reach out and touch the waiting grass
on the homestead but the wind bellowed only in spasms
and the fury of the blaze wedged south toward the cabin
of Tom Freeman, another neighbor, without jumping the
creek. Five hundred bushels of oats and barley were
consumed along with three hundred feet of fencing and
much of Tom's timber before the men could beat the
flames to death. "It's a helluva way to meet the winter. I'd
like to get my fists on the bastard that started it."

"It pert neart clawed into my house and barn. She come
down the hill and took holt so fast I din't know what it
was a'ready yet. I gotta cut wood all over agin, nothin left
to cut from hardly." Scheve complained.

"If you need, come over and take from my timber,"
Freeman offered. He would take a man in for as long as he
needed if it were necessary, and if he had a morsel left to
share he shared it. It was his undoing many times, but it

was his nature to be generous and kind with less fortunate human beings. Though Agnes tried many times, it was a problem she was able to correct only in a superficial way.

Fires extinguished, Dan turned to the Sunday horse race east of town. Agnes cared little for these races, but Dan had a passion for horses and loved to watch them race. Sometimes he engaged in private racing. He had a favorite driving team, a favorite saddle horse, and kept anywhere from twenty to two hundred horses on his homestead at a time. These were mostly saddle and buggy horses from good purebred stock. Occasionally he added a horse or two to his draft team kept for farming.

"Get your duds on, if you wanta see a real goddamned race." Dan was dressed in Sunday best. "It's never too soon to get a boy acquainted with a horse, damnit," he argued Agnes' objection to taking four year old Sam to races.

He would take the boy anyway, she sighed. Why object? She would look up from kneading bread and they would be gone—no goodbyes, just gone.

"Hi, Doc. Come to see a real race, hunh?" Dan nodded, leading the boy.

"Hey Doc, that your boy?"

"Hell yes. Sam."

Old man Roper wanted to shake hands with the lad. Sam found his hand being lifted, wrenched and dropped. The pat on the head. Then he stared into the rheumy runny eyes of an old man gazing at him with a snag toothed grin. He pushed his palsied hand slowly toward the boy. "You Dan Freeman's boy?" his voice quaked like his hand.

Sam stared petrified at this old man shaking under a shag of white hair and let his hand be pumped and his hair be tousled.

Then without warning Sam began to cry and flung himself against his father's long legs.

"You scairt a' me, boy?" The old man tousled the hair again, and Sam pressed his eyes tighter against the legs.

"That boy he scairt a' this ol' man, Dan'l. Ain't that
sumpin'. You daddy an' me knowed each other a long
time, boy. I knowed you daddy whilst he still fightin' rebs.
"Damnit to hell, dry up. This is ol' man Pethoud. Shake
his hand proper. He's the first man plowed a furrow and
turned grass upside down in this whole goddamned Gage
County. Now shake proper damnit."
The adamant boy finally responded dutifully, much to
old man Pethoud's pleasure. "You daddy and me both
kinda firsts. You daddy, he got the first homestead. Say so
right on the deed, by God." He laughed pleased and at last
shook hands with big Dan. "That a fine boy, Dan. Right
fine boy."
Counselors L. W. Colby and Cap Ashby drove up in a
jingling black surrey. Colby was a horse fancier who owned
some racing stock. The race opened with the running of the
finest horse stock around. A short balding man from
Tecumseh nosed his competitors out with Black Angel, a
fiery prancing mare he skillfully clung to. Ashby stalked
off, peeved temporarily at Colby because he'd had to pay
off a private bet between them. "I don't mind damnit, but
you needn't rub it in," he was overheard to say. Colby
laughed loudly, amused at his lawyer colleague.
Dan drank in the exchange, amused and entertained by
his friend's miff. Cap Ashby drew alongside Dan. "It's a
dull damned race, think I'll walk back to town."
"What the hell for? The fun is just about to start." Dan's
face showed no sign of his teasing. "They're gonna run
another race next that'll beat that other race all to hell."
Cap studied the non-committal face carefully, knowing
the impudence and pleasure Dan always got from ribbing
him. Reading nothing in the boring eyes, he ventured a
question. "This a joke of some kind?"
"Don't ask me damnit. Ask ol' Job. The big thing's yet
to come."
"Nag, nag." The crowd began to chant. "Line up the scrubs."

Dan belched a belly laugh, shaking all over.

Cap spat an oath and started the eight miles back to town afoot.

The race of the scrubs ended in the usual brawl afterward among their owners, much to Dan's amusement. Going back to town he caught up with John Bunker's black buggy.

"Race you to the blue," he shouted.

"Yee-ow!" Dan slapped the rein across Spectre's rump in a raucous bellow. The buggy lurched behind the spirited black pony and jolted down the bumpy road swaying from side to side like the pendulum of a slow clock. The high narrow buggy wheels spat grit and dust behind them, the spokes whirred a low breathy melody. Sam braced himself against the footboard and clung to the roof braces. Dan meant to win the race, but he was mindful of the clinging boy at his side.

The river bank halted the flying hooves and jumping wheels. The dust hung in the air as Dan waited for Bunker to catch up. He drew up shortly and without a word they descended the bank. The horses waded the deep water to the center of the river and stopped side by side.

"That's one good horse, Dan," said Bunker admiringly. "Wouldn't want to sell?"

Dan scratched his chin through the wild tangle of whiskers. "Hell no. I'd never get another animal as good again."

Bunker nodded. "You know the horses, ya?"

Dan nodded and tousled Sam's hair. Sam grinned, excited by the harrowing ride. His dad had spirit and he liked it.

"You maybe get the fast one for me, ya?"

"Hell yes," Dan agreed and they moved ahead to soak and expand the other half of the wooden spokes and inner rims tight against the narrow steel tire shrunken by the heat of their race. Inside of a week, Dan had found a spirited gelding for Bunker which proved to be a stiff competitor for Spectre in the occasional races that followed between the two men.

As his term for sheriff neared an end, Dan made no attempt to conceal his dislike for a job he never wanted. Tiring of the demands of favor seekers, he bristled at the law benders who would have him turn his head and favor their illegal requests. He angered them to the point of hostility and open public abuse with his refusals. He convinced L. Y. Coffin, a close neighbor and friend to run for the office. Then he too filed for the same office on the independent ticket to insure a two party bid for the job. "No man should ever go unchallenged," he cried and was to repeat the same belief many times during his lifetime. After Coffin was elected by a fat margin, much to Dan's satisfaction, he busied himself with problems that had arisen during his days as sheriff.

# CROSSING THE FORD

## 1. Before the day of bridges.

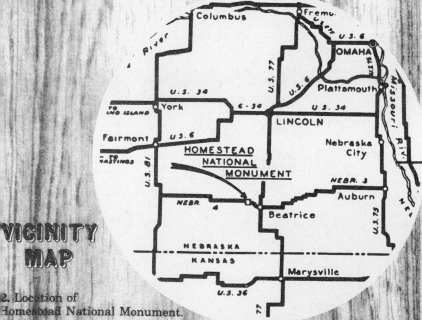

# VICINITY MAP

## 2. Location of Homestead National Monument.

*Daniel Freeman*

*T. Stapaules*

**3.** Pencil portrait of Daniel Freeman with copy of signature.
Portrait by Thespa Freeman Stapaules.

**4. Pencil portrait of Agnes Freeman with copy of signature.**

Portrait by Thespa Freeman Stapaules.

**5.** Agnes Suiter Freeman,
circa 1870.

**6.** Daniel Freeman,
circa 1865.

Courtesy Adelaide Freeman Stapaules.

**7.** The Freeman Family, about 1880.

(Seated): Daniel, Le Claire, George Francis and Mrs. Freeman.
(Standing): Eliza (later Mrs. Daniel Webster Carre), John, James and Samuel.
Courtesy Nebraska State Historical Society.

**8.** Eliza Freeman,
eldest daughter.
Circa 1885.
Courtesy
Mabel Carre Carpenter.

**9.** Samuel Freeman,
with wife Olive.
Wedding photo 1888.

**10.** James Freeman,
circa 1890.

**11.** Agnes May
Freeman.
18 years old.
January, 1908.

Courtesy Nebraska State Historical Society.

Homestead

Recievers Office
Brownville N.T January 1st 1863

Recievers Reciept
No. 1.

Recieved of Daniel Freeman of Gage
County Nebraska Teritory the Sum of Twelve Dollars
Being the amount of Fee and one half the Compensation
of Register & Recievers for the Entry of S1/2 of N W1/4 &
NE1/4 of N. W1/4 & S W1/4 of N E1/4 Sec. 26. Township Four N. Range
Sine East. under the act of Congress approved May 20th
1862 Entitled, an act to secure Homesteads to actual settlers
on the Public Domain

S R Jamison
Reciever

**12. Photo of Homestead Receiver's Receipt No. 1.**

**13. Photo of Homestead Certificate No. 1.**

Courtesy Nebraska State Historical Society.

**14.** Second Log Cabin, sketch by T. F. Stapaules.

**15.** Private Note
from Agnes to Cousin Jim,
1862.

Courtesy Adelaide Freeman Stapaules
(For entire contents, see appendix.)

Samuel Freeman of this city departed this mortal existence at his home on Sunday afternoon at four o'clock of paralysis. He has long been a citizen of Abingdon respected by all. He was born on the 17th day of November in 1805 in Rutland, Vermont, and was in the eighty-fourth year of his age, at his death. Before he had attained his majority he married Miss Phoebe Willis, who was a year his junior. This makes their marital life sixty two years of duration. The marriage took place in Preble County Ohio, and at the fruit of their union seven children were born, two of whom only survive. The survivors are Daniel Freeman Esq., of Beatrice, Neb., and Mrs. Susanah Richmond of this vicinity. Daniel Freeman is a successful farmer, and was sheriff of his county for a term beginning in 1871. The daughter is the wife of Walter Richmond who has long lived in this neighborhood and is also a prosperous tiller of the soil. Jas. Freeman one of the deceased sons was a young man of uncommon brilliancy and was a graduate of Abingdon College. He died at Fort Donaldson during the war while in the service of his country. Samuel Freeman deceased was an upright and honorable man. He was not a proffessor of religion, but was a man of excellent morals, and was both exact and just in his dealings. He believed in the doctrine of spiritualism with sincerity and we have often when asking for his religious creed been met with the reply "do unto others as you would have them do unto you." The surviving wife has much sympathy in her bereavement. It has been her heart's desire for years that she might go first. She is eighty three years of age, and ere many years will join her husband with whom she has lived so long and happily in the spirit world —above.

**16.** Depredations claim against Indian damages, about 1864.

An interesting afterthought was added to the margin of the claim: "and then and there captured took and carried away the (aforesaid) Laura Roper daughter of the said Joseph B. Roper."

**17.** Re-creation of 1887 obituary of Samuel Freeman, father of Daniel.

**18.** Freeman homestead, brick house. Left to right: Daniel Freeman, Lila Freeman, Agnes Freeman, Daniel Freeman, Agnes Freeman, (Quackenbush), Dorothy Freeman...(all three children are Frank Freeman's).

**19.** Inscription on musket: "Taken from British at Benington, Vermont. August 16, 1777. Used by Elkana Freeman at capture of Burgoyne."

The musket was given to Daniel Freeman by his grandfather Elkanah Freeman, and in turn, it was given to him by his father, a Green Mountain Boy during the Revolutionary War, Elkanah Daniel Freeman, great grandfather of Daniel Freeman.

## CIRCA 1900

**20.** Daniel Freeman with trusty musket.

**21.** Typical postcards used by Freemans.

Courtesy Adelaide Freeman Stapaules

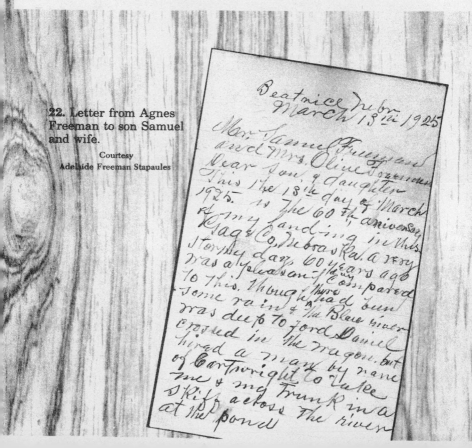

**22. Letter from Agnes Freeman to son Samuel and wife.**

Courtesy
Adelaide Freeman Stapaules

Beatrice Nebr
March 13th 1925

Mr. Samuel Freeman
and Mrs. Oline Freeman
Dear son & daughter
This the 13th day of March
1925. is The 60th aniversary
of my landing in this
Gage Co. Nebraska. a very
stormy day 60 years ago
was a pleasant day compared
to this. though we had been
some rain & the Blue river
was due to ford Daniel
crossed in the wagon. but
hired a man by name
of Cartwright to take
me & my Trunk in a
skiff across the river
at the pond

**23.** Daniel Freeman farm, October 1911.

Courtesy Nebraska State Historical Society.

**24.** Two-room cottage used by Mrs. Freeman prior to her death in 1931. It was erected by son John in 1901 and burned down in 1931.

Courtesy Nebraska State Historical Society.

**25.** Signing the bill making the first homestead the National Homestead Monument site. From left to right: Pres. Franklin D. Roosevelt, Sen. George W. Norris and Cong. Luckey, 1936.

Courtesy Nebraska State Historical Society.

UNITED STATES POSTAGE
1863 1936
3 CENTS 3
DANIEL FREEMANS HOME
FIRST HOMESTEAD

**COMMEMORATIVE STAMP**

**26.** Commemorative Stamp issued 1936 when Homestead was designated a National Monument.

**27.** Granddaughters of Daniel and Agnes Freeman, August 18, 1969 at Homestead National Monument. Left to right: Lila Freeman Angus, daughter of George Francis Freeman; Gladys Freeman Bueoy, daughter of Samuel Freeman; Mabel Carre Carpenter, daughter of Eliza Freeman Carre; Adelaide Freeman Stapaules, daughter of Samuel Freeman. This was the first reunion of the Descendants of Daniel Freeman and Agnes Suiter Freeman Organization.

Courtesy The Lincoln Star, 1969

# V

# The Predators
## 1876 — 1878

Be a representative to the Grand Lodge, I.O.G.T. in
Lincoln? Hell yes, I'll go with E. S. Chadwick. Come
blizzard, hell, or high water the twenty second of January'll
see us there. Nothin' I despise more'n t'bacca, liquor'n
goddamned preachers. You'll see us there. The ignorant
reverend Roberts can warn us friendly or any other
goddamned way he pleases against modern spiritualism, be
it second Sunday after Epiphany or first day in hades. It
don't cut no ice with me. He's runnin' scared a' this
spiritualism, the yella coward is. Nothin' I despise more'n
t'bacca, liquor'n goddamned preachers.

Twenty five thousand acres of Gage County Otoe
reservation lands thrown into the hassle pot. Will James Jay
get it or the B & M railroad? A grab of mammoth propor-
tions. The dinosaur of industry snatching the soil from the
farmer's fingers aided by the local sellouts, the frontier
cottonmouths, the prairie carpetbaggers. While they slit
their brother's throats, they goosedown the barbs of the
opposition for the rapidly expanding monopolies. "A town
that attempts to fight a great railroad corporation, or to
prosper when the interest of the railroad is opposed to it,
stands about as much chance of success as a bull that gets
on the track to fight the locomotive," the fawning editor
of the *Beatrice Express* whined. Lick their boots in exchange for the pat on the head that says, "You're a good
boy, you cause me no trouble." All for the price of being
on the popular side. Never mind the common man, his
labors were meant to appease the rich. This is a tough
country, it takes a tough man to hold her down. We didn't

get here by fawning, we got here by bulling locomotives of
one kind or 'nother on every goddamned kind a' track that
faced us. We bulled our way, mister—don't fergit it. We
grew to be half like the animals we fought. We'll bull the
locomotives too. We cast the dandy in us aside when we
moved toward the prairie. We grew to look like the
weathered sod we turned and the parched grasses we
roamed. We bulled, mister, an' us sod busters'll keep on
bullin' ever where we step. Ain't no turnin' us back—ain't
never no turnin' us back. An' we'll bull the locomotives
too! Dan bulled with the most powerful.

Dan read with satisfaction the account of Cap Ashby's
lecture from the Beatrice Express:

> The lecture on "What Believers Must Believe,
> and Unbelievers Can't Believe," by W. H. Ashby,
> announced last week to take place at the Court
> House Monday evening was listened to by a full
> house. Saxby's orchestra was present to enliven
> the occasion with music.
>
> The lecture was an effort to prove that the
> Bible, as a history and a standard of belief, is
> false, untrustworthy, not divine, not entitled to
> credibility. The lecturer cited several incon-
> sistencies of statement, chiefly from the Old
> Testament, to confirm his views, and in addition
> referred to various Mericles of the New Testa-
> ment to prove the impossibility of accepting the
> Bible as a true record.
>
> The speaker said that the fundamental vice of
> the Christian church is that it makes a merit of
> belief; and for that reason, he was speaking in
> self-defense, as he had felt somewhat the oppres-
> sions of those who disagree with him.
>
> An opportunity was given for reply after the
> lecture, but nobody appearing, a motion was
> carried to form an organization of the "Liberals"
> by electing Dr. Buffon, President. A meeting was
> then appointed at the Court House for tomorrow
> (Sunday) night, eight o'clock p.m.

Dan slapped his leg roughly and threw his head back in
laughter. "Course he has to defend hisself against the
goddamned fundamentalists. Their Christian faith is to
oppress everybody that don't think like they do. If you
don't agree with the damned hell raisers, they try to hang
you. But when they do it, that's 'Christianity'. They lie,
steal, and cheat, hide behind their Bible, and try to tell
other folks how to act. Goddamn, that's purty good. Ol'
Cap's learnin'."

"It's a hard lesson when people get mean with you."
Agnes looked up from her patching. "I feel sorry for
Ashby."

"Hell, he's all right. He's a damned good lawyer and he
can take care of himself. They need to get riled up by
somebody like him. Do the lyin' demogogues some good."

"If people really believed in their religion and lived it, it
wouldn't be so bad. As is, it's kinda disgusting, all right. I
wouldn't get involved in their arguments, though." She bit
the thread loose from the patch.

Dan slapped his leg again and embarked on a new round
of laughter. "Why hell, Aggie, it's the best damned thing
ever struck 'em. Maybe teach some them frauds a' goody-
godies they aren't foolin' everybody. Damned preachers
don't believe in a damned thing they say."

Agnes drew the mending closer to her. Her mouth had
drawn out into that straight tight line. She agreed with her
Daniel, but she never liked these controversies he got
himself into.

Dan sensed her mood and quietly took his Colts from
the hook and disassembled it for cleaning.

In July, the Freemans with their four children left to
visit in Iowa. The little Suiter house had never looked so
good to Agnes and her throat swelled with happiness and
compassion when she saw it. "An' them younguns, ain't
they a prideful sight?" The tears spoke for all of them.
After LeClaire, the same scene repeated itself in

Abbingdon. They found Daniel's parents, older, frailer, and the tears—always the tears. When they returned home, Agnes made Dan promise to make the trip again soon. It was a vow he would keep. Dan was a man of his word. Agnes was a woman to see that he kept his word.

Dan was an expert farmer, and as Agnes remarked many times during their marriage, he made it when others failed because he knew how to do many things and do them well. He was forced to seek jobs that were not so strenuous. A hernia that plagued him during the Civil War was aggravated with age. If he did not do all his farming, he was at least expert enough to direct his hired men. Where he failed, Agnes succeeded, for she was more expert than her husband in managing business and the farm. Most of the credit is due Agnes for their financial success.

Dan bought land, hung on to it while prices were high because the market looked too good to let it go. Prices would slump and he oftentimes found himself in a financial bind that forced him to sell his property cheap. He bought and raised hundreds of cattle and horses and repeated the same poor judgement as he did with land. He doctored many local people, including many well to do Beatricians, but he seldom charged for his services and never tried to collect for them. If a man, friend or stranger, asked to borrow from him, he always shared. If the borrower didn't return the favor, Dan never had the courage or stomach to collect from him. He made mockery of the universal adage for acquiring wealth: buy cheap and sell dear.

He fulfilled the speculator's dream in reverse. He bought dear and sold cheap or else bought cheap and sold cheaper. He was not a man much concerned with finances. He could earn the money well enough, but he let Agnes handle the business end of it. He was an abolitionist turned reformer. He was interested in politics and law and community affairs. When he worked, it was with maniacal persistence, always looking to the reward he generously allowed himself—a trip into town to chin with Cap Ashby and General Colby, a tree planting spree, a trip back east or to Galveston, Mobile, or Hot Springs. But always he rewarded his own labors—partly because he believed life had to contain some sort of personal fulfillment in order to be a worthwhile existence above and beyond the endless task of survival and partly because he was innately restless, easily bored, and seeking always to try to find himself. Medicine, scouting, farming, politics, law, reform, drama, literature, spiritualism, these were exploratory pursuits into his self analysis.

> Dan Freeman has gone into the practice of law. His first case was before the officers of the land office the other day, wherein he shown brilliantly on the defense. Go in Dan.[1]

The defense in which Dan shown so brilliantly was in the hearing on the "Court House Square." The act of 1873 declared the dedication of the square to be valid, ratified it, and declared the title of the land rested in Gage County, even though it was public domain and the Freemans had lived on the lot for two years.

Dan knew his law and knew it well. He knew an act of fraud when he saw it. If it meant going into court or standing on his head to thwart it, he would do it.

He was as complex as his varied activities. His practice of seeking answers was only one segment of the man. He yearned to help his fellow man who might be less fortunate. He burned to have justice done and honesty prevail. He could and did endure much abuse to levy justice where he thought it should reign. He was far more concerned with the right and wrong of a situation than whether it was advantageous to him or to anyone else. It was the principle of the thing—always the principle. Where most men adopt

---

[1] *The Beatrice Express.* May 8, 1873

and live by the code of self interest, they lose perspective
in most other areas, including those which help them to
understand those few selfless men who do not believe in
the dog-eat-dog philosophy of human existence. Wherever
insight and compassion are dwarfed in the balance of
human thinking, the scales invariably tip towards fertile
cultures of hate. Where the simple, selflessness of man
cannot be understood his motives and behavior become the
object of ridicule.

Two months after the courthouse square trial, Dan sold
three lots to banker J. E. Smith for a $4.07 tax deed. Buy
cheap, sell cheaper.

What the hell, work harder and make it up. Old R. P.
Claussen wanted to borrow a book. *Flavius Josephus* would
do him some good if he could understand it.

"Ha. You come you wanta race buggies, hunh?" R. P.
laughed, knowing the horse Dan had gotten for him was
faster than his own.

"Hell yes. But I brought this so's you'd know enough to
get the buggy into the road straight." He laughed spiritedly
and handed *Josephus* to him.

R. P. smiled bewildered. "What's this *Josephus?*
Politics?"

"Read it. See if you can learn something."

"Mebbe I don't want learn this kind. Hunh?" He smiled
again reminding Dan of their political differences. But he
looked about for a place to lay the book. He admired this
man's knowledge of politics and his persuasive arguments.
Finally he propped the book in the window.

"What the hell's the matter? Ain't you got any goddamned place for a book in your house?" Dan was careful
with his many books and kept them shelved and protected.

The Dane looked embarrassed and took the book from
its precarious position on the narrow ledge and placed it on
the table. "I need a desk," he said lamely.

"Jesus Christ." Dan exploded. "You're in one helluva

way." He grinned and sat down to a morning of arguing with the bewildered R. P.

The court house block, now better known as Freeman's square, would soon be legally Dan's by squatter's claim. When it was, he would have to be moving back onto the homestead. He was eager to move but had been giving a lot of thought to building a better and bigger home for his growing family. There was plenty of good clay for brick. The right technique and he could mold his own. He read every written word he could find on brick molding. The growing season this spring of 1874 was good: plenty of rainfall, early spring, the black soil responding to the plants. A perfect season.

The crops were all planted. All they needed was a load of wood from the homestead to keep Agnes in cooking fuel and he could settle down in earnest to brick making. The homestead air filled with singing meadowlarks and whispering grasses was exhilarating. The ax swung steadily, the wagon filled, the sun warmed the cool earth. A small boy trudged the rough road from town towards the homestead. Joe Graff drew his horse to a halt beside the boy. "Hello Sam, goin' out to see your uncle?"

Tom Freeman, no relation to Daniel had moved into Coffin's homestead while he moved to town to carry out the duties of sheriff. Tom Freeman was a veterinarian farmer from South Carolina and "a hell of a good fella if he only had a little more sense." Dan had once declared.

Sam shook his head. "My Dad's cuttin' wood on our claim."

"Oh. Din't know dat. You pert small boy to go on such a long walk alone."

"I'm seven." Sam said proudly.

"Ya. You big boy, Sam. Pert neart growed." He grinned. "You be careful, now."

Sam drew himself tall at the words and summoned courage to tell the man. "Tom Freeman ain't my uncle anyways."

But Joe Graff was already bouncing down the road on his plow horse.

As young Sam approached the east hill of the homestead he came onto the camp of Big Nick Kinnamon, a Scotsman from Beatrice with a dozen or better horses corralled with a rope and three hired hands stirring beans for dinner over an open fire.

Big Nick walked towards the approaching boy and asked, "And who are you?"

"Sam."

"Sam? Are you hungry, boy?" He watched the boy eye the beans. "You wouldn't be Dan Freeman's boy?"

Sam nodded. "He's my Dad."

"Well," he boomed. "Pull up and have some grub. It's as free as the water in that there crick to any boy of Dan Freeman's."

Encouraged by the big burly man and the smell of beans, Sam accepted the tin and sat down to listen to the stories of Big Nick.

Did he know the little Cameron Boy? He was Big Nick's nephew. Just died yesterday of a contagious disease. Would he tell his Ma?

Yes, he'd tell his Ma about the Cameron boy and watch her face turn pale and the tears roll across her cheeks. He was a gentle child, she would say, then resolve to go pay a visit to the dead child's mother.

Sam licked the bean gravy from the tin and handed it empty to Nick. He promised to eat with the big men again sometime and proceeded across the hill to the homestead where his Dad was finishing loading the wagon with wood.

On the way home, Sam mounted the high stack of wood and rode proudly beside his father. His dad never scolded him and usually backed his boys in whatever they wished to do. After the wood was unloaded, Dan picked up four straight green walnut logs he'd laid aside and threw them back onto the wagon bed. He drew up sharply in front of

R. P. Claussen's house and called for Claussen to come out. R. P. peered from the half open door. Seeing it was Dan, he threw the door wide and came out. Dan threw a log into the yard with a mighty heave, frightening Claussen aside. The second, third, and fourth flew through the air with equal force. Dan brushed his hands and squarely faced the man. "Here's your goddamned desk. Solid walnut. All you gotta do is make it." Without another word, he grabbed up the reins and sped down the road. After many years of curing, a table was finally made of the logs by a descendant more ambitious than R. P.

In August, when some of the wheat was in the shock and the ears were milky on the corn, dark clouds came up from the west and north, hovered for a while, then descended with champing gnawing fierceness. Billions of grasshoppers in droves, in clouds, in five hundred foot deep platoons invaded the prairies. Their clacking gnawing jaws were as consuming as a crackling prairie fire. Anything that was chewable was eaten; the crops and grass first, then the buildings and fences. The only reason entire buildings were not consumed was solely because the lure of greenery over the next hill prodded the insects on. When they left the corn and beans in stubs they moved on making room for the next cloud, the next invasion. When there was nothing left to eat, they ate each other. But still they came swooping down, covering the ground three inches deep in places.

Farmers tied strings around their ankles holding their pants legs tightly closed to keep the hoppers from crawling up their legs. Women threw bedding over the gardens hoping to save the food they were depending upon. For the hopper it was no deterrent, simply an additional feast. They ate through sheets and blankets and then devoured the gardens. They beat against the roofs of houses like hailstones and broke tree limbs under the weight of their numbers. They invaded barns eating harness and pitch fork handles and hoe handles. They crawled into houses through cracks under the door and around windows. When the doors were open they ate bedding and curtains. For many homesteaders these invasions were so traumatic, especially to the women, that they rapidly threw a few belongings into a wagon and tried to outrun the hoppers. For some, the experience was so frightening that it drove them out of their minds and made raving lunatics of them.

Trains on the U. P. near Kearney, no longer able to keep schedules, were content if they could do more than sit and spin wheels in grasshopper juice.

The scourge of the hoppers' presence was debilitating enough but it could in no way equal the long term effects of their hit and run visit. Many farmers packed what few possessions they had left and went back East. There was no crop to winter them, no grass to winter their live stock, and no garden to supplement their tables. Government relief for grasshopper razed farmers was slow in coming, acutely short funded, and soon exhausted. It was a choice of packing up and leaving or floating a private loan from a bank or mortgage company at the exhorbitant interest rates that ran from 24 to 100 percent. There were far more wagons going East than coming West this year and three out of every five homesteaders were unable to hold onto their claims. Any man who hoped to repay his debt on the strength of the next crop usually failed. Unless he'd lived five years on his claim, he couldn't mortgage his homestead. So the man who mortgaged his crop was in precarious shape and in good line for foreclosure on the unmortgageable homestead.

Many farmers were forced to plow under their wheat and plant corn in the same year. But these were more fortunate than the farmers in eastern Nebraska whose crops were invaded late and could not manage a second crop that season.

Despite the state aid which came in the form of food

staples for relief, the suffering was acute and many people continued to succumb to the pressures of indebtedness. Gage County received some flour and a carload of corn to help alleviate the plight of its people.

Wash Rogers declared that the only way a man could make money that year was to move to Minnesota and bag grasshoppers for the fifty cent a bushel bounty they were offering there. "The only damned trouble," Henry Odell reminded him, "was gettin' the ornery critters to set in the baskets fer ya long 'nough to collect the bounty."

If the insect predators were not enough to break a man this August, the human predator was. While Dan and Agnes were gone with their children down into Missouri to drive back a dozen work mules, Hiram Webb, the county treasurer, issued a warrant for sale of the Freeman house, privy, and fence for taxes delinquent on lots other than the lot the house stood on. No notice was given in the paper, he simply sent his hireling, Michael Lynch, a deputy, to move the Freeman house containing all their household belongings, their privy and fence into Court Street to be auctioned off to the highest bidder and delivered to the buyer. Webb had waited until the Freemans were gone, having known in advance where they were going and for how long because Dan had brought promissory notes amounting to over $300.00 face, and all due, to Webb before he left to be asked for by the county treasurer and applied to the taxes due on his other properties which amounted to less than $200.00 Webb took advantage of Freeman's absence to expedite his trickery. He placed the promissory notes which were given to pay the taxes due aside. It was Webb's chance to show his loyalty to the speculators who had burned under the fast move Dan had made that beat them to the wanted spoils. This particular situation also afforded Webb the chance to make some extra money.

The auction took only a few minutes because no notice

had been posted and no mention by word of mouth was made. It was done secretly, under public guise, and with the legality of a public county office by bonded elected officials. The house, with household goods, privy, and fence were sold at a token price of $102.00. The actual value of this personal property was conservatively placed at $870.00 by Freeman. As soon as the house had been sold, Michael Lynch, Webb's deputy, and George Dorsey, Webb's disillusioned and angry friend, drove to the premises of Freeman's homestead and seized seven hundred bushels of wheat and three hundred bushels of barley which Lynch sold to Dorsey amidst guffaws and wise cracks for a total of $118.44. This was done under the guise of a public official operating through a public office for purposes of applying the sale money to the so-called delinquent taxes held by Freeman. The market value of the grain was one dollar per bushel valued at a total of $1,000.00 for the thousand bushels of grain that Dorsey took. Lynch, acting under Webb's orders, and Dorsey were the only people who entered Freeman's premises under the guise of public auction. The only other party was Dave Byers who was acting as tenant and hired man on the homestead for Freeman and living there. Byers tried to prevent the two men from taking the grain, but they threatened and intimidated him into submission. While Webb claimed in district court later that his actions were guided by his intense feelings against Freeman for taking "Court House Square," Dave Byers swore that Webb and Dorsey were bragging about their plot to get even with Freeman because they did not like him and because they wanted to "see the cock taken down a notch or two when he found the stuff missing." Byers was instructed to play along and not tell on them. He did so, until they left, out of fear for his life.

Fraud, oppression, and corruption were filed by Dan when he returend home to find he had none. There was no place to put his family on the homestead either. Dan and

Agnes had driven the mules directly to the homestead
by-passing Beatrice, having crossed the Big Blue River at
Blue Springs. Dave and Sarah Byers met them at the corral
and explained the situation with Webb and Dorsey.

"Christ a' mighty, Dan, I never knowed what was goin't
on. Took you house and outhouse clean off'n the ground
and sold 'er. Damn if she don't beat hell."

Agnes looked so distressed that Sarah took her to the
house. After the initial shock Agnes began to anger. "You
get Hardy and then the both of you get the sheriff." She
told Dan.

"I will, goddamnit, but first I've got to find a place for
my family."

"No need. You stay right with us. We'll gather our
b'longins t'gether and leave you be with the cabin." Sarah
was insistent. "Won't be more'n tomorrow and we kin be
out. Mrs. Freeman and me kin make do with one night
t'gether."

Agnes was grateful to this big woman and made no
protest.

"Sons-a-bitches," Dan swore and tore down the road
astride the gray mare for Beatrice.

They quickly built a cabin across Cub Creek on Dan's
own property to house the Byers so he could move his own
family back into the log house.

Dan and Agnes were grateful to Dave and Sarah for their
loyalty and, though the Byers would have moved to let
Agnes with her brood of young ones have a home, Dan
insisted on paying his debt of gratitude by building them
the house.

When the case came to the district court the sympathy
of the court was with Webb and Dorsey even though
evidence was presented to show the properties Webb had
levied delinquent taxes upon against Freeman were properties which had no delinquent taxes due or properties which
did not even belong to Dan. Evidence of the grain stealing

and Dave Byers' testimony was ignored. Evidence of the
promissory notes due and face valued at more than any
taxes Dan owed was ignored. Evidence that Webb had kept
the promissory notes himself and never applied them for
taxes was ignored. Evidence that the money collected for
selling the house, privy, fence, and 1,000 bushels of grain
was unaccounted for and never applied to any delinquent
taxes was also ignored by the Gage County Court.

Evidence that the block of land the house sat on was
free public domain when Freeman squatted it, was not
legally the possession of the city of Beatrice, and that the
personal property of a man is not detachable from his real
property again was ignored and cast aside. Justice and the
court had become a weapon of personal opinion. Justice
was a word not a fact for those who knew the rules and
played the correct game with the right cohorts. And so the
court rendered its decision in favor of the county commissioners and against Daniel Freeman.

Years of hassling brought the case to the Supreme Court
of Nebraska in 1879 where the petty politics of local bias
and unreasoning prejudice could not penetrate—a place where
a decision could be based on the legal code of the country.
Decision was passed in which the following facts were
established. The "Court House Square" was legally a part
of Gage County, thereby free public domain when Freeman
built upon it; that the city of Beatrice had never owned it,
had no legal right to it, had never dedicated it, thereby
having had nothing to ratify. That the house, privy, and
fence had been illegally removed from the premises since
whatever is annexed to the realty thereby becomes part of
it; Freeman had lived on the land long enough to own it by
squatter's right; that the county treasurer Webb was a
trespasser in his actions in selling the house, privy, and
fence; that it was evident to the State Supreme Court that
the real object of this case was not to collect any delinquent tax, but to obtain possession of the premises; "it

may fairly be questioned whether Gage County has any title to the block in question. A dedication was made by the town authorities for a particular purpose, but, so far as appears, the county has not applied it to that purpose. That a dedication can be made by parol there is doubt, but it certainly is necessary in some way to prove the acceptance on the part of the public." (A courthouse had already been built in 1870 on Cropsey's addition for Beatrice). "The plaintiff was peaceably in possession of the premises and could not be divested of such possession in the manner attempted in this case. The judgement of the district court is reversed, and the case remanded for further proceedings."

Further proceedings included litigation which continued through most of the 1880's as it had the '70's. Judgement and damages were brought against Webb and Lynch who persisted in insolent and unwarranted personal attacks upon Dan. In 1881 a judgement for $458.00 plus $182.00 interest was issued against Webb. Litigation failed to yield the damages from the insolvent Webb and no settlement for damages for Dan's house, privy, fence, and 1,000 bushels of grain was ever made. Even litigation to get back the promissory notes which Webb held privately was necessary. Feelings among the principles involved ran deep and bitter after that. Dan often said, "Everyone knew who the goddamned frauds were and what they were after from the beginning. Right means nothing to most people."

The theft of Freeman's property, the lack of damages, the costly litigations and the bald arrogance and cruelty which he and his family were subjected to during this time prompted Dan to reverse his original intention of turning the lot back to the city for a public school site. He was bitter, angry, and harbored great resentment even though the case was settled in his favor. He would forever despise Hiram Webb, George Dorsey, Michael Lynch, E. M. Hill, J. F. King, Joseph Graff, and William Lamb, who had sought to bring their personal hatreds to bear against him in this case. Other members of the commissioners he had sued had been brought into the case primarily because of their position, not their actions. These he could tolerate with the help of time, and did.

Stripped by the grasshoppers and bled by the human vultures all in the same summer, the Freemans faced a bleak and threatening winter with Eliza, Sam, James, John, and Agnes again in a "family way."

It was a winter of slaughtering much of the livestock to survive and mortgaging property and lots and living on short rations. But Dan had been a good provider, and they were spared the desolate defeat of returning to Iowa or to Illinois. Dan, stalwart defender of man against frauds, would not allow himself to leave while he kept watch over this group of county commissioners.

Baby Dan was born in the winter of 1875 in the midst of a vicious winter to a staunch family weathering the wounds of a grasshopper plague and human inflicted deprivations. His beginnings were not altogether the strongest.

While acting as director of the school board, Agnes had secured the services of Ollie Grant to teach the Blakely township school. She would board with the Freemans and teach from the different homes, rotating the days. She was Sam's first teacher. Ollie was a lovable, bright young woman who imbued her students with great enthusiasm for learning where before they had remained aloof and adamant towards school. She was to influence many children, including Samuel Freeman, with her contagious spirit for learning. Ollie was a welcome addition to the Freeman household. She gave Agnes the intellectual stimulation she craved and made her days brighter and more endurable.

Despite the setbacks of the summer before, courage flowed deep in Dan and Agnes.

"I'm gonna get Seeman Ripley to come down from Chicago and teach us how to make bricks. Good bricks.

We've got the best damned clay soil in the country to do it with." Dan told Tom Freeman and Joe Suiter.

"He's been in Nebraska before showing people how to make and fire them and since we've got the soil right on our own places it's only logical we use it."

"I'm agreed, Dan." Joe said.

Tom nodded. "Since he's not costin' us much, I say the sooner the better."

"A brick house with smooth floors?" Agnes was radiant. "Just like back in Iowa."

"Just like back in Iowa 'cept a helluva lot better," Dan's eyes twinkled. He hadn't realized it before, but this was the first building of a dwelling that had aroused Aggie's enthusiasm. The life had been hard for her. The strain was showing in wrinkles about her mouth that had been drawn that way so long that they'd set.

Seeman Ripley would come by train to Beatrice. From Beatrice he would ride buggy with Dan and quarter with the Freemans. He would have Ollie Grant's bed, now that school was finished for the term.

"Ripley is a Quaker gentleman," Dan cued his family. "He speaks in the Quaker ways and dresses in the Quaker fashion. His son is the president of the Rock Island Railroad. I want you to remember he is a gentleman and I expect you boys to be gentlemen too." The seriousness of their father's tone conveyed the message carefully and indelibly to the children. Dan changed to his best suit to meet the train without Agnes' prodding and the weight of the guests' visit was properly impressed upon the family.

The children watched bug-eyed from the window of the cabin as the Quaker gentleman dismounted from the buggy. His severe dark dress and hat and his notched cane were awesome to them. When he shook Sam's hand, "I am most pleased to greet thee" and tousled his blond hair, Jim reached the limit of his control. With a snicker muffled behind clenched hands he ran from the house and to the barn.

"Bring him back," Dan ordered Sam. He'd never seen his father so strict nor so quietly angry before.

With some prodding after they'd both had a good giggle, Sam managed to drag a reluctant Jim back to the house. Fortunately for Jim, the intervention of Seeman Ripley had calmed Dan down enough that he gave no more than a severe look to the small boy. Agnes exhaled a sigh of relief and turned her full attention to the roasted prairie hen and white biscuits. With the boiled potatoes and turnips steaming on the table, the meal began.

"We've got the finest clay in the country," Dan explained to Mr. Ripley. He produced a hardened brick of raw clay for Mr. Ripley to examine after supper. They guess-weighed it in the palms of their hands. They probed with a knife and examined the filings close to the lamplight.

"I believe thee has," Ripley answered Dan's claim. "It be indeed fine brick soil."

The matter of bricks was settled for the evening and the two men entertained Agnes and the children with stories.

> Once, coming up the Mississippi, a fellow passenger was injured by a horse on board. As he lay on the deck all the passengers filed by expressing great sympathy. One fellow who was most concerned and anxious faced the crowd and shouted, "just how sorry be thee? Be thee sorry fifty dollars worth? If thee be, I'll put up another fifty." Soon they had collected enough to give the young man a good start in life.

Dan liked the dignified man and his witty jokes. Ripley was eager to teach the men the art of brick making and watch them start their own.

Dan worked quickly forming the brick and firing them as fast as he could form a load for the kiln. His house took shape rapidly with the help of Dan Cable, a good carpenter.

A. P. Hazard drove into the yard late one afternoon. "Dan'l," he boomed above the baying hounds. "The one day I thought sure as hell you'd be ta town." He laughed as he watched Dan walk briskly to the buggy.

"It must be somethin' damned important for a sidewalk sheriff to come all the way out here to find me." He leaned against the buggy wheel.

"Oh, it's Green. He's filed a warrant agin' a fellow he's accusin' a' stealin' a couple a' Otoe ponies from the reservation."

Dan nodded.

"You're 'sposed to try 'im, bein's you're Justice of the Peace, first thing in the mornin'."

Morning came and Dan found himself listening to a scared fuzzy faced kid accused of horse thieving. He had two Indian ponies all right and no bill of sale, but he swore "clear to hell and back agin'" he never stole them. He bought them off a fellow near Endicott, he argued, and hadn't even been near the reservation.

They were Indian ponies and little else mattered to the man called Indian Agent who seemed enamored with his title. When he pressed charges, he wanted action and most of all to keep his ledgers meticulously balanced.

All Dan had to decide was whether there was sufficient evidence to find the fellow guilty. If there was, he'd be bound over to the county and jail. Colby and Hazlett defended the accused thief, both relating the number of incidents in which Otoe stole from Otoe and sold the horses they stole. "It is a common occurence, as Major Green well knows," Colby argued. "That there is also much inter-tribal stealing is also well known."

Dan found no real evidence against the man and very little circumstantial evidence. He declared the man innocent of the charge and dismissed the case. Colby and Hazlett each took a pony from the defendant for court fee.

Green left uncontrollably angry. He instructed the Otoe to "lie low till dark, then steal your ponies and clear out." Which they did. The courts and law obviously were mere words to the Indian agent who espoused their value on one occasion, but contradicted law and order on others. He interpreted the law freely as he so chose, even to advising stealing. Had the law not been interpreted so broadly and loosely, he would have found himself faced with serious problems for his retaliatory advice.

"He's just sore and mean actin' out for the local big shots over this Court House Square case," Dan said. "In other words, it's just his goddamned Christianity seepin' outta him, that's all." With that he dismissed the man.

The hoppers were sparse this summer and the wheat crop the best it had ever been. Dan had winter wheat the length and breadth of the Cub Creek bottom land. The wheat was the finest Dan had ever seen. He came in and announced to Agnes quite unexpectedly in August, "I'm going to enter my wheat in the Centennial Exposition in Philadelphia, by damn. I'll thrash two or three bushels and take it back to the world's fair. Damnit I've never seen finer wheat."

Agnes examined the hatful of berries he'd brought to the house. "It sure is fine wheat. Won't that make some bread, though," she said admiringly. "A person could live off of this and be well fed. My, what wheat."

"Then you don't mind?"

She shook her head. Why should she mind? He was proud of his crop and his work. He took pride in everything he did. She thought it fine if he took the wheat to the world's fair in Philadelphia, besides he'd do what he wanted, anyway.

Dave Byers moved onto a homestead of his own west and south of the Freeman homestead and no longer had time to hire out to Dan. Consequently, Sam, though only nine, had to help run the Marsh reaper with his father. When they finished reaping, they set the bundles head up in shocks which dotted the homestead like squat grass huts.

The Gascoign brothers, with their big threshing rig that required six teams of oxen to operate, threshed for Dan.

The threshing operation required about twenty men to work from daybreak until dark, after the shocks had been hauled into a central location and stacked during August. Threshing always took place after the fields were cleared of the grain, plowed, and broadcast seeded again, and other work was done in the fall.

Dan hauled wheat to Black Brother's elevator in Beatrice with two or three teams of oxen in a big blue army wagon with a flared top. The elevator was made so the oxen drew the wagon up a high ramp and the men scooped the grain from the sloping rear of the wagon.

Later, Dan boarded a train for Philadelphia with his bags of wheat and entered it in the Centenniel Exposition. He came back to the homestead beaming with pride, carrying the first premium ever given on winter wheat at a world's fair.

Sam continued to herd cattle on horseback on free range southwest of the homestead up into December. All the neighbor boys had their herds there as well and they spent many of their days visiting and playing, in between bringing back leaders that strayed or lead the herd away. At lunch time, the boys all gathered round Sam to trade their cornbread for his white bread. He was the only boy with white bread and he hated it. They felt they were getting a bargain to get his white bread in exchange for their cornbread because they disliked cornbread. Early in November Sam began to shake and chill while herding cattle. He was forced to bring his herd in early. He was scarcely able to corral the herd and crawl to the house, he was so feverish. Agnes put him to bed with heavy blanketing and called Dan to come in from the barn.

"Sam has ague." She nodded towards the bed.

The rocking bed and blankets re-affirmed her diagnosis—the sweaty forehead, the chills and jerking. Quickly they worked to make the mixture and brew it: prickly ash bar, Peruvian pine bark, Ceyenne pepper brewed with brandy.

Four doses a day for a few days and Sam was cured.

The brick house was at last completed and they were able to move into it before cold weather. For Agnes it was a thing of luxury. It was solid and warm and she hoped it would eliminate the recurring attacks of St. Vitus dance in James caused by his rheumatic fever, and the ague in Sam and John.

Since the neighbors were still financially troubled from the grasshopper rage of the summer before, it was their habit to send people who wanted work to Dan. His mammoth wheat crop had helped him overcome his reverses but more than this they knew he would always give a needy man a job. Daniel Coates came to the homestead by this route. He wanted work enough to send him a ways further in traveling throughout the country sight-seeing. He was first cousin to the J. & P. Coates mercantile magnates. Daniel Coates was a big man in his late forties with a big greying beard. He carried his own shot gun and shared his quarters with a big red Irish setter. He wore a pack to wrap around his middle with Quail hooks festooned to it. "He's a congenial man, a good hunter, a hell of a story teller, but a damned poor farmer." Dan said of him. But a month's wages for exchanging stories with Dan primed him for his next sojourn and another job, and he left Dan rejuvenated until another traveler would stop.

Dan had made more than enough brick for his house. When the house was built, he made more and sold them all, including the broken ones. He could have sold all he could make, but the gnawing began and the urge to move on to other things crept over him. He repeated a pattern. Once he conquered a problem or situation and had it well under control, he finished with it and moved off to conquer another obstacle. The intensive work; the reward. Many times he rewarded himself with books: Tennyson, Scudders medical texts, or Byron. He devoured the speeches of Robert Ingersoll, and imbibed in his philosophy of "Enjoy today—without the regret for the loss of yesterday or the fear of tomorrow." He accepted Ingersoll's philosophy on death, "I do not fear death anymore than I fear sleep."

Dan admired Ingersoll's oratory and eloquence and his fearless stand in politics. As Dan tired of the hard physical work, he longed to involve himself in politics. This was his reward for hard work, his "today to enjoy."

This time the reward was a trip to Iowa in the Spring of '77 with his team and wagon. He would spend a month doctoring along the way to pick up extra income for debts incurred in building the house. He managed to chart his trip to include LeClaire and Abingdon, Illinois. East of the Missouri River he came upon a slight, white haired man walking spritely toward his wagon. "What in the hell you doin' Grandad Suiter?"

The old man stopped. Recognizing Dan, he came up close. "Goin' to Beatrice to see my daughter, goddamnit. What the hell you doin'?"

Dan slapped his thigh and laughed heartily. "That's a helluva long ways to walk. Get in, come on back to Illinois with me and ride out to Beatrice in the wagon."

The old man shook his head. "Druther walk. T'ain't far." Without another word he passed the wagon and gave Dan his back. He was a frugal man and had always walked wherever he needed to go. He felt no special need to ride now in spite of his advanced years. He arrived in Beatrice, by foot, had his visit and left for Le Claire before Dan came home. When the brick house was finished, Sam had written to his grandpa Suiter, "Come visit us and bring grandma." Grandpa had obliged, but without grandma.

Dan drew his rig into Rockford at noon and stopped at the livery. While unharnessing his team, he overheard a couple of young toughs plotting to rob him when he came back from dinner at the hotel. He found an iron, hid it in a chink in the log wall of the stable and went to his meal. Returning to the stable, he noticed three young men lolling

about the door. He went in, picked up the iron he'd
hidden, walked to his horses and began harnessing them.
One of the three men entered the livery, closed the doors
behind him and came up to Dan with a pitch fork in hand.
"I bet you think you're quite a fighter don't yar? I seen
yer bag ya carry with ya. A man that pertectin' mus' have
sumthin' awful important in it."

"All you have to do is come take it, if you can."

The words angered the man and he lunged for Dan with
the fork. Dan slung the iron at his head and with the blow
knocked him unconscious. He strode to the door, flung it
open, and called to the two waiting outside. "Come get
your goddamn fighter so's I can drive my team outta here."
He turned and drove his team rapidly across the floor as
the two hoodlums scurried to drag "Mat" to safety.

Later that summer, Doc Dan again went doctoring into
Texas. He came home with a herd of worthless burrows
driven by boys he'd hired. Though the animals were of
little monetary value, Dan's sons were enamored with them.
They were compatible companions for Sam and his 13
hounds. Sam and Jim were so eager to show the stubborn
gray jackrabbit-eared arrivals off that they mounted a pair
bareback and rode them into Beatrice. As they rode down
Court Street, Buck Buchanan and Ole Clarke both older
than Sam, rushed into the street and began wrestling with
Jim to dismount him. Sam raised his whip and struck Buck
hard across the face. The two boys lunged for Sam and
knocked him from the burrow. Orin Stevens had a hotel
and livery stable on the side of the street. He'd seen the
boys attack the Freemans.

"What the hell's goin' on?" He bellowed from his
doorway. Ole and Buck backed off. "You leave those
Freeman boys alone and get the hell outta here, 'fore I get
my horse whip."

Ole and Buck turned and ran down the street and
through the back of Claussen's store. "You boys a' right?"

Stevens called to Sam and Jim. With their nod, he went back into the hotel. He was a special and close friend of Dan's and he wouldn't allow anyone to molest Dan's children.

Dan hung his medical diploma on the wall on the left side of the east door above his deed for the homestead. On the second floor he had a library walled with books, and a walnut table with a kerosene reading lamp. He spent much of his time in this room and it was on such an occasion that he read the election returns for county commissioner in the *Beatrice Express*. He noted the puny 180 votes his neighbor Scheve pulled for commissioner, and observed, "and he's not even an infidel, by god."

Otto Schmidt drove into the yard riding high on the wagon seat. The baying hounds announced his arrival and drowned out his reception. Dan cursed the yapping dogs and their noise and walked up to the wagon. Schmidt had helped Dan break sod with a team of oxen the year before. After a few brief amenities Schmidt asked. "tought mebbe I collect my bill, ya?"

"I'm short as hell on cash, but I'll give you that big black colt down there in the corner of the lot."

Schmidt's eyes followed the finger. "I don' no. Mebbe I don't like him so much, ya? I tought da job she wort' more dan dat."

"That colt's worth a helluva lot more than the bill I owe you."

"I see. I see Dave Byers, see what he say." He slapped the rein across the skinny brown mare's ribs and drove out. Dave Byers' wife was a Bennett and first cousin of Dan's. She got along well with the Freemans, but she sometimes had difficulty in keeping Dave straight. He was "all right," Dan said of him, "except his lack of good sense and his fear that everyone he dealt with had cheated him."

Otto Schmidt found him in such a frame of mind when he told him Dan had offered him the black colt for his wages. Dave advised him that the colt probably wasn't worth it and to hold out for greenbacks. Later Byers bragged to Tom Freeman of his advice to Schmidt.

"I thought you'd ought to know what Byers done," Freeman explained his visit to Dan.

Dan was amused. "Listen Tom, you tell Byers what a valuable animal that black colt is. You're a vetinary, he'll believe you. Tell him the goddamned colt's worth three times Schmidt's wages but not to let ol' Dan Freeman know it or he'll take back his offer."

"I'll sure as hell do her, Dan." I'll have the bastard runnin' up here with his tongue out fer fear he'll lose that horse. Just leave it to me, Dan. I'll fix ol' Byers and Schmidt both and you'll get your debt paid off." Tom rode off, a smug grin playing across his face.

Dave Byers lost no time in repeating Tom Freeman's praises of the big black colt to Otto Schmidt. Only a day after Dan and Tom's plan, Schmidt rode up bareback on the same hungry mare. "I bleeve I take dat dere black colt, Dan. T'ain't wuth m' job, but I'll be satisfy," he lied.

Without a word, Dan took the lead rope Schmidt had brought and went to the corral for the colt. He'd out-plowed Schmidt's team of oxen 3 to 1 with his own three fiesty ponies turning that sod under, but never mind, this would pay the German off, and it was a hell of a good joke.

Agnes snorted when Dan told her Schmidt had taken the colt finally. "Ah, shoot. He's like all the Germans, clannish and suspicious" Agnes despised the Germans for their clannishness. She came from Hessian ancestors, but her father's family had broken with the Germans altogether and her feelings carried much of the intensity of her father's.

Agnes was taking over more of Dan's medical practice each year. She had delivered some eighty homestead babies since her arrival in Nebraska. She read every medical book Dan owned and subscribed to a medical journal for further information. She enjoyed doctoring and helping her neighbors in their times of trouble. She had the reputation of being "Mrs. Freeman the ag-yoo and baby doctor." She was especially skillful with children. As she had taken over this part of the practice, Dan had confined himself more to the treatment of social diseases, specifically venereal disease. It was a disease he found patients for both at home and on his wanderings into the south. He had devised a secret medical concoction of his own which he applied in his treatment. It was a remedy which would be handed down to his son James who Dan hoped would continue to carry on the medical practice in the family. Though it was the practice in early medicine to hand down secret treatments from father to son, and though Dan wanted James to use it, his interest in the field was short lived.

Dan's treatment of social disease was a mixed blessing to his family. While he made good money treating many prominent Beatricians who stole to his home only after dark, he also suffered the ridicule of the town. He was dubbed "the old clap doctor" by many. Some of his patients who crept to him in the dark for treatment would loudly taunt him with the "old clap doctor" title in daylight when they could find an audience. They knew Doc Dan never divulged secrets of his patients, so they felt quite secure in their daylight harassment. It "eased their burden of guilt some," Dan often said. "But who gives a damn. It's a game in town now. The ones that talk the loudest are considered the guiltiest by the crowds. So who gives a damn?"

But Agnes cared. She found it disturbing to have ridicule thrust at her noble Daniel. She pleaded with him to stop the practice and often thought she had succeeded until on some dark foggy night the hounds would start baying. The yellow light in Dan's east study window guided the man from the hill. A rap on the door. John would open it. "Dad," he yelped up the stairs, it's ol' Davey. He's got the

clamps. Hurry up, Dad, ol' Davey's got the clamps all over
the place." And Agnes knew she could not stop him from
seeing the man. She knew the taunts would go on. He
would be known as the "old clap doctor."

"Mrs. Rose came over today. She just moved in up the
creek a ways. Was a nice woman had a beautiful little girl
named after her. They came all the way from Indiana."

"Get them into the lyceum, Aggie. Get acquainted
quickest that way."

"I asked her. She wants me to come over next Wednesday. I'll enjoy it. She's a lonely woman." Agnes hurried the
supper. "Where you going?"

Dan stopped in the doorway. "Thought I'd go over see
cousin Wib Rogers."

"Tonight's lyceum at Rogers'," she pushed the string of
hair behind her ear.

Dan scratched at his beard, saw he wouldn't be able to
get out this time, turned and sat down. "Damnit to hell
anyway. A man can't go anywhere in this damned house."

Agnes turned back quietly to her stove. She stirred the
mush irritably thinking of Dan's curtailment, practically the
only one ever imposed on him. Her mouth drew straight
and tight in that angry line. By supper, Dan was joking and
teasing as usual. His anger had dissipated in a short time.
Agnes' anger had seethed and magnified until she could
only sit at the table and glower in a silent clump of wrath.
Either Dan didn't notice her mood or was careful not to.
He said nothing unpleasant and espoused many unnecessary
pleasantries. Agnes seldom got this angry, but when she did
the Gods thought twice before acting and so did Daniel.

By the time they'd jogged in the buggy behind Spectre
to the Rogers homestead, Agnes had relaxed the severity of
her lip somewhat and Dan relaxed enough to drop the
pleasantries and simply keep a furtive eye out for her.

It was election night and the success of the lyceum
depended upon the stability of the officers voted in. It was

a late March evening with a few spring bugs flitting through the air giving a hint of warmth to come and winter to go. The neighbors were jovial and relaxed this evening. T. Dolen spoke to several in the group seriously and secretively. They supposed he was campaigning for himself. Ann Rogers took Mrs. Rose and made the rounds of the women, introducing the new neighbor.

When Tom Freeman brought the meeting to order, he said, "I'm 'bliged to say what a festive air the evening has. We should have a extry good program and we'd ought to convene early bein's election's tonight." Even Joe and Will Barnhouse were there. They didn't come often, but they were made welcome even though their old mother admitted they weren't quite right in the head. It happened when she "was carryin' Joe first. An Indian attack that scairt the hair clean onto the top a' my haid. And then agin with Bill I hadda run and hide under a wagon when a bull charged me. It were enough to make the poor boys looney headed," she said, notwithstanding the fact she'd never known an Indian when she carried Joe, and as T. Dolen once said, "she sure as hell never knew what a bull was."

The election would take precedence over the program Tom announced. The office of President was up for nominations. T. Dolen stood and gave a five minute speech on the worthiness of the office, the need for qualified leaders, and the general gravity of the job. He ended abruptly by nominating Joe Barnhouse. There was a titter among the women, a few stunned expressions, and Joe Barnhouse's beaming round baby face bristled with a sparse black growth across his cheeks and chin. There was a clamor to close the nominations and vote. Somebody threw in old man Gascoign's name making the nominations legal. There was a flurry of counting, snickering, and obvious fun in the group. No one was surprised when Joe Barnhouse got all but three of the votes.

When the fun was over, Tom Freeman had the job of

righting the situation and going about the voting seriously. He was more than a little bothered in how to tell Joe he couldn't be president. Nathan Blakely saved him from the ordeal. "Now we've had our little joke, lets start the nominations for president. I nominate Wib Rogers."

No one had counted on the hurt look on Joe Barnhouse's face. "How come?" He sputtered. "Ain't I the president?"

"You started this whole thing T. Now you straighten it out." Tom, a little disgruntled, dumped the matter square in T. Dolen's lap.

T. began to squirm uncomfortably. He didn't see any escape so he called Joe and they stepped outdoors a moment. When they came back in Joe stood up and announced indignantly, "I'll quit, but I won't resign," much to the hilarious amusement of T. Dolen. When he sat down he leaned over and asked T. "did I do that aw'right, T.?"

The crowd laughed at T. and he squirmed shamefaced in his chair. The joke was over with a backfire. Dan laughed for years at the joke. "I'll quit, but I won't resign," he'd repeat and laugh all over again.

Wednesday came and Agnes was looking forward to visiting Mrs. Rose. Most of the women neighbored by walking from home to home, but Agnes was adept at harnessing a pony and hitching it to the light buggy. She trotted Julie along the rough road to Rose's and hitched her to a post outside the log house. Mrs. Rose opened the door, a tearful somber woman. She fell into Agnes arms sobbing. Her little Cora had just died a few minutes before from diphtheria. The tragic impact of death again. Agnes tried to steel herself against it, but somehow the hurt always crept through her armor. She went in, examined the child, then made it ready with blankets and the little corncob doll on its breast. Its hair was smoothed then covered with the corner of the blanket. Finished with the

child, she went to Mrs. Rose. "You've cried enough now.
Busy yourself, scrub the house down with boiling water
and lye soap. Use water and ashes to scrub the floor. I'll go
home and bring you some henbane so you can sleep
tonight." She hurried to the standing horse and buggy.

The scrubbing was both therapeutic and disinfectant for
Mrs. Rose. The father buried the child with a neighbor's
help and Mrs. Rose gratefully went to bed after taking the
henbane Agnes brought her. Agnes repeated to Mrs. Rose a
well worn phrase she often used, "time is the healer. Give
yourself time." With that she left the grieving woman.

Beatrice was featuring a fire and brimstone religious
camp meeting week along the Blue river. Dan decided to
take his family and attend one. He tried all the churches at
least once, seeking to learn if one had an answer the others
didn't. He'd tried the Presbyterians last week and didn't
care for the damned preacher McMeen. Apparently nobody
else did as they had a new preacher already by name of
White. Agnes knew he'd have to try the new one too. The
only preacher he'd ever seen that was worth a damn, and
he wasn't worth much, was the First Episcopal's first one,
Rev. Clarkson. The only reason he cared for Clarkson was
because he'd once said, "the ministers don't know the
answers. Many think they do, but they don't. Only God
has the answer." Dan agreed with him fully that the
ministers didn't know a damned thing. He disregarded the
mention of the higher power. He believed there was a
creator of sorts, else how did anything get here? "But if
there's a God walking around, I want to see it. I don't
want no goddamned preacher just a telling me it's there."

The camp meetings turned out to be a fine place to visit
your neighbors all at one time, and the social side of them
was pleasant enough to almost make one forget what the
roving circuit rider had said.

Johnny Greenwood taught school in the new brick
building Tom Freeman had built west of the homestead in

1878. He farmed in between teaching on a claybank farm between Plymouth and Hoag. The clay was good for bricks but not for farming and if Johnny wanted to make a living for his wife and baby he'd ought to go into brick making and sell off that clay bank in red squared chunks, otherwise he'd starve to death sure. But Johnny didn't think so. He taught to support the one thing he loved to do and that was farm. If the only place he could afford to do it on was a claybank, well, damnit he'd farm the claybank. Anyway, it wasn't none of the neighbors business. Though he didn't think so, Johnny Greenwood was a far better teacher than farmer.

Diphtheria continued its hop skip pattern over all of Eastern Nebraska. Gage County was plagued by the dread choking disease that would touch down on one or two in a family, skip the next one and dive onto the third. Little Danny Freeman was the victim in his house. Dan and Agnes worked over him day and night until he fought off the fever of the sickness. He was getting better and able to sit in his high chair to eat when he choked to death. Agnes ran to her three year old Danny during breakfast unable to clear a breathing passage in his throat. She felt him go limp then stiff and cold before she let Dan wrap him tightly in a blanket. Dan called on Wib and Wash Rogers to help him bury Danny. Mrs. Rose came to Agnes, trying to comfort what she knew was impossible to comfort in a person stricken this way.

Eliza twelve, Sam eleven, and Jim eight grieved openly for days for the small boy they had become so attached to. Young John was the bewildered one. Too young to understand, to know. Few words were spoken for many days. No one talked about the death. As was their custom they drew the hurt inward silently.

Finally Agnes pushed the tragedy aside, drew her mouth straight and grim, and buried the hurt deep within her next to that other one placed there when James Freeman died at

Fort Donelson.

When Johnny Greenwood's baby died of diphtheria a day later it became a different problem. Dan was called to help subdue the irrational Johnny who went berserk when he picked his baby up and it no longer breathed. He became so distraught that he smashed the baby's high chair with his bare hands, took the ax and chopped the cradle to pieces, and finally attacked his wife and tried to choke her to death. Though they buried the baby in Johnny's claybank, Johnny was never right again and he had to leave the claybank he loved to farm and the school he taught to support the claybank.

# VI

# Land and the Railroads
## 1879 — 1888

In 1879 a new treaty was drawn up with the Otoe and they were removed from the Gage County Reservation to the Indian Territorial Reservation in Oklahoma. Thousands of acres of fertile grazing and farm land would become available after the railroad dipped its quota through the center of the former reservation. It was to be the end of Indian attacks and scares and the frontier woman would no longer live in fear of her life insofar as the Indian was concerned.

Cap Ashby formed a combine of prominent business and professional people to bid on the reservation land. Dan Freeman was one of the members of the combine. The business enterprise was good in theory, but when Cap with two or three trusted cronies stacked the bids and bought off the auctioneer, the matter became one for the federal government to handle. The plan was to auction the parcels of land to the members of the combine at a token figure of ten to twelve dollars per 160 acres. If anyone else bid on the land the auctioneer was to keep the bidding going so high the person could not afford the land and would back off. Occasionally the bidder didn't back off and ended up paying as much as $200.00 per acre for their land. The scheme, devised as a combine with a number of members buying together to get a bigger chunk of land through their combined buying power, was actually confined to a small active group who secreted their actions from the other members and got the auctioneer to lead the special maneuver.

Dan Freeman, upon learning of the trickery within the

combine stated, "Law practice is a good thing if the ones who practice it do so for the benefit of the common man. But if they practice only to make big money and to become influential they're the lowest goddamned scoundrels of all mankind." With that, he wrote Ashby off as an enemy and a cheat never to resume even so much as a conversation with the man again.

If Ashby weren't enough to get a man down, Dan fumed, some ignoramus like the editor of the *Lincoln Journal* was. "Lickin' backsides to sell copies of his paper." Dan stormed. "Imagine anybody being so impudent as to say the farmers would be as out of place in administrative offices in the state as hogs in a parlor. Who the hell he think he is?" Townsend's rumbled under the attack of bushy faced Dan. Many other men who didn't feel anything like hogs in a parlor because they farmed fumed right alongside Dan. The die had been cast, the division was there. The distinction became clearer between the working man and the monopolies, the farmer and the politician, and the distinction was resented. "When a man riles another enough, he'll up and do something about it, make no mistake." Dan warned. "And damnit to hell, I rile fast."

He followed closely the labor movement in the east, the embryo of what would develop into the populist movement. He saw need for farmers to organize into a Knights of Farmers just as labor had organized into the Knights of Labor. "It will come," he predicted to the men in Townsend's. "It will come."

In 1878, Dan was forced to sell at sheriff's sale to make settlement for a debt to W. E. Ryan. The lots auctioned were number 2 in block 15; 4 in 50; 1 in 60; 2 in 60; 10 in 75; 11 in 75, all in the city of Beatrice. On his farm the following livestock were auctioned: 3 brown mares, 8 or 9 years old; 1 brown mare, 3 or 4 years old; 1 bay horse pony, 8 or 9 years old; 1 white cow with roan neck; 2 red and white spotted cows; 1 red and white spotted steer; 1

yoke of red stags; 12 of the largest white hogs; and 20 of the largest black spotted hogs.

On the 31st of March, 1879 George Francis was born. He was named after the author George Francis Train who Dan found interesting. Though he was named George Frances, he was always called Frank.

In 1879, the city of Beatrice voted bonds in the amount of $20,000 to bring the Omaha and Republican Valley railroad from Blue Springs to Beatrice. The bond vote was hurriedly done without fully and properly informing the voters of the city whose property was being levied against for the bonds, what getting the railroad involved.

Dan owned eleven lots in Beatrice at the time and objected to the methods used in levying the bonds and to the coercion brought upon the taxpayers by the railroad company. Besides Freeman, W. L. Rogers, and V. S. Whittemore asked for an injunction against the Omaha and Republican Valley Railroad Company until a thorough investigation could be made. Charges made were that the votes on the bond issue were improperly canvassed. Instead of two disinterested parties canvassing the votes, two people well known to be supporting the bond issue did the job. They were Emory and Drum. The voters were not informed of the votes cast for or against, the rate of interest that would be levied on their taxes for the bonds, the rate of payment, nor the final payment date. The bonds were to be issued to the railroad company upon completion of the track ready to run passenger cars on the 31st day of December 1879. Certain specifications were required of the tracks and roadbed to qualify as a satisfactory job, i.e. "The said railroad was to be of uniform gauge with the Union Pacific railroad and shall be maintained and operated as a first class railroad with passenger and freight depot at said town of Beatrice . . ."

The plaintiffs averred that:

The railroad by-passed Blue Springs by one half mile, the grade of the railroad was irregular, uneven, and imperfect. The ties were so completely and negligently put down that it was extremely dangerous to run a train of cars over said road, that in many places the ties were scattered very wide apart and many of them did not touch the ground at all but were suspended by the rails and they otherwise laid loosely on the frozen ground and not fastened in their places in any manner except by having the rails spiked to them. Said road was not ballisted at all and no attempt made to ballast it. Many of the bridges and culverts were temporary structures and very imperfect. The railroad was thus imperfectly constructed and in great haste in extremely cold weather and upon the frozen ground in order that the said company might be enabled to run a train of cars over it by the first day of January 1880, and thereupon act up a claim to said bonds and thereby fraudulently procur the said county commissioners to issue the said bonds to the said railroad company.

Freeman obtained the injunction which he sought against the railroad. A similar charge against the same railroad had been made three years earlier in Saunders County. H. D. Perky was charged with asking for $10,000 to use his influence to get people in Saunders County to vote bonds in the aid of the Omaha and Republican Valley Railroad. Between 1862 and 1871 alone, Congress granted 135,800,000 acres of free land to the railroad companies to encourage railroad construction, a mass that nearly equaled the total area of the thirteen original colonies. Despite the free land gifts, graft seemed an inevitable element in their development.

Agnes' niece, Aggie Richmond, came out to the open prairies of Beatrice this spring. Her first comment was, "Law. A person can look farther and see less in this

I'd go mad with the loneliness of it. How'd you ever stand it, Agnes?"

Agnes smiled at the small slight shouldered woman. "It wasn't easy at first, but now it's my home." "A sea of grass," she had first called it.

"I spose," Aggie said, unconvinced. "I can imagine the women out here work like the horses to keep from being lonely."

"It's a damned good way of gettin' some work out of them." Dan waited for her reaction.

"The country hasn't changed you any, has it?" She liked Dan, but some of his rough ways chafed her lady like disposition.

Dan laughed uproariously at her remark. He knew he'd crawled under her hide. He respected Aggie Richmond, but there was too much of the lady in her for him to resist teasing. He thrived on teasing, probably because it was the way he knew best to show affection when he liked a person. If he didn't like them he would also tease, but it would be a raw personal and insulting type of harassment.

Agnes was grateful for the company of this favorite niece. Aggie was always level headed, knew what to do in an emergency, and kindly efficient. She was intelligent and stimulating to talk to. She did a good deal of public speaking back in Abingdon. There were few things this small woman did not know. Frank had fallen asleep in Aunt Aggie's arms as she rocked rythmically in the cane rocker. Agnes pulled the dasher from the churn with short quick flicks of her fingers. She searched the shelves and boxes muttering to herself as she went.

"What in the world you lookin' for Agnes? You sound like a clucky hen."

"My butter mold, my butter mold," she sang back gayly preoccupied. "I 'spose the kids have been playing with it again. I wonder where they've put it." She paused to think.

"What the hell difference does it make? You don't need any damn pretty design on the butter. All we do is eat it anyway," from behind the newspaper.

"Well, I like a mold anyway. It pretties the table up nicely." Agnes was irritated with Dan.

"Well, Jesus Christ, if it's a mold you want take Frank's pants down and set his rear in the goddamned butter and get your imprint."

"Why, I never heard anything like it," Aggie snapped horrified. "How could you make remarks like that about a small child?" She demanded angrily.

Dan laughed heartily at Aggie and recommended she take a dose of Indian herb bitters. She was miffed over the remark for days. It took an evening at the opera house with Faust and Marguerite and Dan's best behavior to woo Aggie back to herself again.

A two wheeled emigrant cart stopped at Cub Creek for water on the way east from dry Kansas. They drove a yoke of cows hitched to the cart and had four hungry looking children squatting over the few crowded belongings in the cart. Dan asked them to stop at the house and take dinner with them. They went to the house reluctantly because they had no money for a meal. When Dan reassured them that he didn't charge for meals, the youngster's eyes lit up in anticipation of food. If Dan brought hungry children to eat at Agnes' table, she was so overcome with compassion she invariable sent extra food along with them. This family left with the whole batch of fresh bread Agnes had just baked wrapped in clean cheesecloth. As they drove out of the yard, she hurried to scrub the tobacco tainted dipper, and dump the contents of the water pail. She was angry with the man who had slobbered the stinking horseshoe juice and cud into the dipper. She could tolerate many things, but never chewing tobacco in her drinking water. Finally she was able to busy herself with a new batch of dough.

She was elbow deep in it when the dogs began the
baying and yelping. From the door she could hear the
threshing of horses in the creek bed down by the bridge.
Hurriedly she went after Dan on the hillside with his apple
trees and called him. He hadn't heard the ruckus. He didn't
hear much anymore. When they reached the bridge they
found John Scheve, his wagon, and team in the bottom of
the creek. The bridge had collapsed and slithered to one
side. They got John out and Dan was cutting the harness to
free the horses when Henry Odell came up. Between them
they pulled the broken wagon out and got Scheve and his
team home. "I told dat Lamb, dis bridge she gonna go
down, but he say, no. She strong as hell." He shook from
shock and the soaking he'd gotten in the creek. Dan had
been after the commissioners for some time to fix it, but
they were still fighting him from the Court House Square
case and wouldn't listen.

When Agnes got back home she couldn't find John. She
thought he'd been with Dan on the hillside but Dan hadn't
seen him and supposed he was in the house. When Sam
came home from plowing, he was sent out to find John.
About dark Sam came bringing John home to a very
worried mother. "He's been over to Odells," Sam shoved
him into the house. "Had supper and everything."

"You shouldn't take supper with Odells. They have a
hard enough time feeding their big brood." Agnes
reprimanded.

"I know," John said excitedly. "Mrs. Odell kept belly-
achin' to the kids. Eat some more bread and butter, Jim
and Willis. We only got a dollars wuth a beans. Made me
lose my appetite, 'sides the beans was hard."

"Never mind that," Dan snapped. "Why the hell'd you
go off without tellin' your mother?"

John began to cry. Agnes saved him from a good shaking
from his father. "Why did you go, John?"

"Well, cause Jim Odell coaxed me off."

Agnes wouldn't let Dan shake her John, so he stalked angrily from the house at her interference. It was a habit she repeated often, protecting the boys from their father's watered down wrath. But she could never stand to see them punished. As a result they often used one parent against another to get their way. Agnes had seen children mistreated often and she was always careful never to maltreat hers, even in regard to the work. She didn't want her boys to work "until their bones were set," or "until their muscles have developed sufficiently that they won't break out with a hernia." She didn't want the girls to wash dishes "because it will spoil their hands for playing the piano." Somehow she became more mellow with the younger children than with their older siblings. Eliza and Sam had been brought up to work and had done a fair share of it. But after these two, she became much softer with each succeeding child. Perhaps their father's age affected the interest he showed in them. He was nearly seventy when his last child was born and he admittedly became weary of disciplining the young ones after he got older. Between his age and Agnes' loose standards of lenience he found himself relinquishing more and more parental control to her. He even found himself leaning more heavily than ever upon her judgements. It was unfortunate for her younger children that her discipline was so slack, but fortunately her business judgement was sound. Had it not been, the empire of 1,480 acres of land and other holdings would never have been built.

Midsummer, Dan walked up Cub Creek to look for a couple of roan calves that were missing from the pen overnight. A mile up the creek he came onto Joe Graff thrashing about in a poison ivy thicket. He was out of his head and nearly dead. He brought Joe into the house and doctored him. He used strong lye soap to neutralize the poison ivy and gave him fifteen drops of chloric ether in a cup of water. After Joe began to come out of his daze Dan

took him home and gave him some sugar of lead to bathe
the poison ivy affected parts of his body for the next few
days. Joe cried pitifully and clung to Dan's hand when he
left him at his home.

That same summer the Freeman family had a visitor.
Loretta Freeman, Dan's twenty year old daughter by his
first marriage, came to spend part of the summer. Dan was
delighted in seeing the girl he never expected to see again.
The children welcomed her eagerly and accepted her immediately. Agnes was somewhat reserved and aloof at first.
She had never talked to Dan about his first marriage and
she had not spoken of it to her children. The gay Loretta
was soon called Etty by the family and Agnes was as drawn
to her as were the children. She was full of interesting
stories for Eliza and mothering to the younger boys. She
was eager and helpful in the household and made friends
easily in town. Mart Rich was especially attracted to her.
He drove out every Sunday in his buggy from Beatrice,
oftener if he could manage, and the two went buggy riding
across the prairie. When it became apparent that Etty was
beginning to get serious about Rich, her father was
troubled. He had doubts about Rich. He felt he was not
the man for Etty. He made his feelings known to the girl
and she listened politely. A few days later, as Dan was
coming home from Beatrice, he met Rich going back to
town from a visit with Etty. Dusk and an old man's eyes
failed to see the girl curled up on the buggy floor hiding
from her father. Under the buggy box lid lay her satchel of
clothes. When they heard from Etty again, she was married
to Rich and living in Kansas City. Dan forgave the young
couple for eloping and answered her letters. The corre-
spondence went on for several years until after a long
silence Dan received a letter from a preacher in Kansas City
asking for money to take care of Etty. Dan became so
angry that Etty had become involved first with Rich and
then a preacher that he refused ever to answer or to

consider her his child. Etty had gone as mysteriously and quickly as she had come.

When Sam was seventeen, he made a trip to St. Joseph, Missouri driving one of three wagons to bring back apples. Wib Rogers and his son Crozh drove the other two. It was Sam's first trip and a deliberate initiation into the ways and pleasures of travel and wandering that Dan introduced him to. He wanted his boys to learn to do as many things as possible and above all not to be sissies. Dan told Sam, "It'll be a good lesson in politics for you, goin' into goddamn bushwhackin' country like St. Joe. You'll get a real sight into them around there. It's the natural habitat of scoundrels like Jesse and Frank James."

His father's word proved true, and Sam and the Rogers met many southern sympathizers and several northerners who had been maltreated by the predominantly Dixie City of St. Joseph. Most valuable of all in his father's mind, Sam became acquainted with that stirring restless feeling that only wandering salves.

The frequent visits to the homestead by young Webster Carre were climaxed in March of 1884 when Eliza and he were married in the brick house. Eliza had three new dresses for the occasion, a navy blue with black velvet trim, a gray satin with blue velvet trim, and a third of coffee colored crepe. The young accountant took Eliza to Beatrice to live.

The void made by Eliza's marriage was filled seven months later when Agnes gave birth to LeClaire, named for the home town Agnes longed so many times for. Lee, as LeClaire was soon called, was the sixth son born to the Freemans.

Ten years after the great grasshopper invasion, the reputation of Nebraska as an inhabitable desert was proved a myth. It had become a prosperous farming land well supplied by rainfall and receptive to the millions of alien trees brought and sunk into the soil. Typical vegetation was describable only as heavy and lush. Nowhere east of the Missouri did plants grow so luxuriantly and so plentifully. The farmers were prosperous and businesses were more prosperous. Typical of the luxurious products of Nebraska was William Jennings Bryan, a man gifted in the pre-World War I diplomacy of extravagant praise and oratory. He became a symbol of radical thinking in the late '80's with his backing of the new populist movement. Dan was glad to find so capable a man championing the cause of the common people. He traveled to Lincoln, Omaha, and Kearney to hear Bryan speak. "It's a new era," he told Agnes happily. "The era of the common man. We will not be put down. The world will look to us common people as its future. It can't be any other way." He declared. "The powers of the kings, their thrones, and the caste system will go. Billie Bryan will help us see to that. You'll see, Aggie, You'll see."

'86 was a bad year for storms. There was plenty of rainfall, in fact, too much. There was flooding on both the Big and Little Blue Rivers. Livestock was washed down the boiling streams never to be seen again. Tornadoes dipped down in the middle of the prairie and skimmed along, unobstructed for miles, wreaking havoc and death until they spent their fury. Hail storms that beat in roofs and rendered range animals senseless plagued the farmer.

In February, 1887, Dan received word that his father Samuel had died. He left Agnes in charge of the homestead and boarded a train for Abingdon. Sister Sue would need his help. When he returned, he was somber and quiet for months. He spent much time in brooding.

After his father's death, he became more conscious of his original application for the homestead and the significance of the legal number description on it. He proudly displayed the deed which had had little significance to him before. While Agnes gave little thought to the title of first home-steader, more pleased they got the land than what the deed read, Dan was justly proud of his deed. In 1886, he sent a cane cut and whittled from wood on his homestead to Galusha A. Grow with a letter which read:

> My application for said patent was No. 1, my proof of residence No. 1, and the patent is recorded on Page 1, Volume 1, of the records at Washington. Hence this cane sent you was grown upon the land first taken under the said Homestead Act.
>
> Knowing well that the zealous and able efforts put forth by you to secure the passage of said act justly entitle you to be considered its father; and realizing that said act is the greatest that has ever been passed by Congress, I feel that I, as one of its benefactors, am not overstepping the rules of propriety in presenting you with this simple token of my gratitude and appreciation. Begging you to accept this simple Homesteader's gift, I am, most respectfully,
>
> Yours, Daniel Freeman

Some years after the passage of the Homestead Act. Grow spoke before Congress upon the beneficence of the act and remarked that there were two interesting incidents connected with the passage of the bill. First, it took effect on the day of Lincoln's emancipation proclamation, second, the first settler to benefit from the homestead bill was named Freeman. After briefly citing the circumstances of the first filing on a homestead, Grow said, "I trust that the last of its beneficiaries in the long coming years of the future will be a free man."

Dan was justly proud of the letter of acceptance which he received from Grow, thanking him for the sturdy cane made by a sturdy breed of man, who had helped open up the plains and prairies for the country.

Never long removed from a court case, Dan was either plaintiff or defendant. The two or three cases in which he sought Supreme Court action ground on over periods of ten to fifteen years per case. Other cases he became involved in were the standard recovery of money, clearing titles, transfer of real property, settlement of boundary disputes, and foreclosure cases. When the territory was being settled, there were no clearly defined laws and going to court was the only means a man had of establishing law and precedent. Dan's thirty or forty litigations over a period of forty years may seem excessive to an observer today, but for a man involved in as many enterprises as he was, the number of court cases certainly did not make him a litigious figure. Rather, based upon a study of the cases and their nature, a researcher is impressed with the number or precedents he helped to establish.

Once he'd taken a case to court, he did not always pay his attorneys their fees. In some cases he felt they should contribute as much to the welfare of the people through the law as he had. In other cases he would become angered at the attorney, pay them a pittance and tell them they were not only "not worth a goddamn" as an attorney, but that the token fee he had paid was "more than they were worth." Albert Hardy had taken the Court House Square case against Hiram Webb through district court and later the State Supreme Court for Dan and won. Later, he took the case against the Omaha railroad in which Freeman finally compromised and received $3,500.00 over and above court costs and attorney's fees. Suing for what he considered to be due him for past legal services, Hardy asked for a judgement of $1,339.65 and costs with interest. Dan had paid Hardy a total of $73.10 for the sum total of his services over a period of sixteen years. "In answer to Hardy's petition, I deny each and every allegation except one. The sum I've paid Hardy is well and above what he's worth."

The court saw it somewhat differently and asked Dan to pay $44.90 in cash, pay off a note and interest of Hardy's for $100.00, and each party to pay their own court costs in this case as settlement.

In the '80's, the Mennonites began to settle around the homestead. They brought much aristocracy and autocracy from their native land. They looked upon themselves as the landed gentry and expected everyone else to treat them accordingly. They wore their traditional black garb and drove big black teams right down the center of the road. Anyone else using the road was expected to get out of their way when they met, even if it meant removing themselves completely from the road itself. When the Freeman boys met the Mennonites they refused to move which greatly angered them. If Dan met them, he invariably pulled over stopped and spoke politely to them, then drove on. When it came to respecting another man's belief or point of view, he was always a gentleman. He never made an issue where nothing was to be gained from it. If there was no principle involved, then compromise was the better part of judgement in his estimation and he applied this rule of thumb in everything he did. As a result, Dan got along well with the Mennonites. Agnes could never be quite so broadminded. She disliked the clannish autocracy of them and felt they were undemocratic. She was polite with them, but disagreed with them on principle.

In the winter of 1888, the blizzard that rendered most of Nebraska helpless erupted. It caught men out on the prairie unprotected and herds of cattle far from shelter. Even many of those that had shelter froze or starved to death before feed could be uncovered for them. Buffalo froze to death in big neat rounded herds. Children were snowed in at schools, or lost and frozen trying to find their way home in the blinding storm.

School was still in session in the brick Freeman school when the blizzard struck with its sudden fierceness. The teacher had the good sense to hold the children in the school and carry in a good supply of wood from the woodhouse to keep the stove burning. It was nearly dark at

four o'clock, and Dan, disturbed at the appearance of the
sky, called Sam into his study. "I 'blieve you better take
up your fiddle and go up to the school and stay until this
blows over. It'll comfort the teacher to have a young fellow
there as well as the younguns. Not to mention how John
and Frank will feel to see you."

"I better walk. Any horse'll freeze to death."

Dan nodded.

Sam hurried to wrap the violin safely from the blowing
snow and wrapped his face to protect it from the wind. It
was only a quarter of a mile to the school house, but
keeping on course through the blinding snow taxed the
keenest instincts in this boy. When Sam entered the school
with a jolly laugh, the worried looks on the children's faces
mellowed some. John and Frank were immensely pleased
that their big brother was there. The big gunny sack of
food, mostly loaves of white bread and a big square of
butter with enough dried beef to flavor some sandwiches,
that Sam brought was frozen solid when he opened it up.
Worry and fright had made the youngsters hungry. With
Sam Freeman there, his fiddle close to the stove to warm
the gut strings brittled by the freezing air, the youngsters
began to ignore the howling wind and the darkness that
settled in the room. There would be no sleeping this night
with temperatures that froze ice six feet from the hot pot
bellied stove. They would dance to the fiddle music, march
around the room and clap cold hands, but they would stay
awake and do as this handsome mustached young man
directed. There would be no freezing or panicky children in
this school tonight. *Darling Nellie Gray*, *Nellie Blye*, *The
Arkansas Traveler*, *Beautiful Dreamer*, *Yankee Doodle*,
*Sutter's Rag*, and many others sawed against the cold of
the room as Sam tweaked and grated against the strings
through the endless hours of the long night. Children who
lolled or yawned were hustled along in line and tempo by
the teacher in shifts. They were allowed to sleep an hour

close by the stove, then they were up circulating for an hour while the others slept. "The water bucket. Time to put the water bucket on top the stove, the ice is forming on the top again." And so the night wore on and the following day. Towards evening Fred Roper, Henry Bennett, and Dan Freeman waded the deep drifts on horseback, leading riding horses and carrying blankets to wrap the children in to take them home.

The harsh winter gave way to a mellow gentle spring. The meadows gurgled with running snow water and the dormant grasses greened beneath the crusts of slow melting snow banks. For the first time, Beatrice was billing the Chautauquas.

It was this spring that old man Ford and his young son cut down a bee tree on the homestead and took a tub of honey from it. When Dan found out about it, he ordered Sam to hitch up his team to the buck board and follow him on horse. Dan meant to trail and find the man who had come onto his place and destroyed the bee hive. At the west edge of Beatrice they found the team and wagon they were looking for hitched behind a barn. Dan drove into town for the law while Sam entered the barn. Old man Ford offered Sam five dollars for the honey when he was confronted. "If your daddy wants more, I'll pay him." But he never offered a reason for coming onto the Freeman place and sawing down a tree.

Dan was angry enough to make him go to the jail to do the settling instead of making a settlement behind the barn. It was more legal this way, and the affects would be more lasting. He accepted another ten dollars from Ford, glowered a bit, then allowed him to be released.

L. W. Colby bought Zeizefoan, Turkish for Linden Tree, in partnership with Dan Freeman for $10,000. Colby invested the greater share in the thirteen year old Arabian stallion presented to President U. S. Grant by the Sultan of Turkey several years earlier. Grant in turn gave the horse to

his son who later sold it to Colby and Freeman. With a fine
stallion like Linden Tree they expected to raise fancy race
stock. A race track was set up on the west edge of town on
Colby's land. This land later became Linden Tree Park
named after the stallion. Though the horse was a fine show
animal, he was something of a disappointment to the
owners. His disposition was sometimes hostile and threatening and he often engaged in spirited fights with other
stallions. he required more than normal disciplining, but the
blue-gray was probably the finest trotting horse in the
country. When Linden Tree died, he was buried royally in a
straw lined grave in the center of Colby's Linden Tree Park.

Jim Ladd who owned Counsellor, a world record holding
trotter, lived two or three miles east of Beatrice. Dan was
never happier than when he was working with horses or
watching horses race. It was a passion with him. He would
often go out to see Jim and talk horses, or Jim and Looie
Riesen would be at the homestead talking racing. "The real
trouble with your old Linden Tree was the fine breeding.
Any horse with such fine breeding gets skittish and
temperamental." Jim explained the stallion to Dan. "A man
has to really coddle one a them spirited thoroughbreds."

"Oh, hell. The only thing wrong with that horse was the
training he got. Whoever first trained him didn't know a
damned thing about a horse. He roughed him and made
him skittish. If you want a gentle animal you have to treat
him gently."

"Well, I don't know. My old Jetty was a gentle animal,
and you know how rough Hank was on him till I got onto
him about it."

"Hank didn't starter train Jetty, either. It's the first
trainer that counts, I think." There was no end to what a
man could think up to talk about horses.

Agnes called from the doorway. They were ready and
waiting for Dan to bring the rig around to the door.

"Mattie must be finished, Ma's ready." Dan laughed.

Mattie Tice was often called upon to sew becoming dresses for Agnes. She liked to dress up and ride to church services in the carriage with Dan and often found herself just a button or hook and eye short of having her clothes ready to wear. Mattie would then have to work frantically to get her into the finery on time. She worked with a mouth full of pins and unintelligible clucking as her finger's flew. Dan remarked that they could never go anywhere without Agnes having to make whatever she wore from scratch. He liked to tease her about this, although Agnes vigorously denied it even in the midst of doing it.

That evening the baying and yelping began with the high pitched yipe of black Shep mingled between. "Why it's the editor," Dan greeted the man genially. "Come in."

Some time was spent in congenial visiting before the editor began to fidgit and hesitantly start sentences he couldn't finish. Finally he said, "I need some medical advice for a friend."

Dan took him to his second floor office and closed the door.

"I have this friend," he began, then laughed nervously. "He thinks he might have the social disease, you know, the claps. But he's too scared to go to a doctor and find out. You being a doctor and specializing in this kind of disease . . . . Well, I promised I'd come talk to you and perhaps get some medicines that would prove helpful to him." He wiped his forehead with his shirt sleeve. "You understand, he's just too nervous about it to talk with anyone and I thought I'd . . . ."

Dan leaned back in his chair, thumbs drawn through the buttonholes of his jacket.

"You do understand, don't you?"

Dan nodded seriously. "Why don't you just pull your britches down, editor, and show me your friend. It'll make it a helluva lot easier for the both of us." He rose to get the kit he used for such purposes, and withdrew the box of secret salve.

"I don't do this much anymore. My wife'd a helluva lot
sooner I quit. In fact, I have quit, mostly."

Without a word the editor complied with Doc Dan's
request. He stole back many times after dark to gratefully
receive the treatment with congenial amiability. When Doc
Dan met him on the street in Beatrice after that, however,
the editor was taunting and hostile if he had an audience.
It was again at this point in Dan's career in social diseases
that Agnes complained. She asked him to stop treating the
disease saying, "I'm sick and tired of you being called the
old clap doctor."

"Oh, hell, Aggie. Only the bastards that got it and want
to hide the fact call me that."

"No. It's not only them, but that's not so important. I
won't have you help people who turn on you and belittle
you after they've got the help."

After a long silence Dan yawned tiredly and answered. "I
'spose you're right. I'm getting tired of it anyway. It's
mostly the married ones that have it and they're worse
about paying than anyone else." With that he stopped
treating venereal disease and reduced his medical practice
altogether. It gave him more time to spend in town arguing,
discussing, and visiting.

His absences during the week soon prompted Agnes to
answer Frank's query, "Your father will stay home and
work this Sunday. There's nothing doing in town that day."

One day Orin Stevens asked Dan, "Why the hell don't
you just move to town, Dan? You're here ever' day
anyway. Save you that trip."

Dan laughed. "Goddamnit, if I moved to town I
wouldn't have no damned place to go."

In the middle 80's Dan had two hundred head of fine
durham cattle and over a hundred head of saddle and
driving horses. He had many offers to buy, but he set his
prices too high and discouraged sales. In the panic of the
nineties, he was forced to sell them for seven dollars a

head. These were the same cattle that Sam had earlier herded on public range where a neighbor had cut out eight of Dan's herd and driven them home with his own. When Sam went out to round up his cattle, he found them missing. He discovered them in the neighbor's yard and had to threaten with his blacksnake to get them back. When he got them home and told his Dad what had happened, Dan was so confused he rushed to the house for Agnes' advice on the matter. He would have let the neighbor have them rather than fight over it. But Sam was not his father and the old was giving way to the young. Sam smarted under the insolence of remarks by the neighbors of "injustice of the peace" when his Dad was serving as Justice of the Peace and "infidel" because Dan questioned the practices of organized religion and the bigotry of church members. He intended to take none of it. The white haired, white bearded figure was a fire-eater of old and his son aimed to keep and strengthen that reputation.

Sunday, the Odell boys came over. It was raining so they joined the Freeman boys in the house repairing bridles. Dan was working in his library above them when the boys got overly loud and rowdy. Though Dan was hard of hearing, the noise so angered him he rushed down the stairs swinging his cane in the air and cursing one volley upon another. His eyes blazed, his beard quivered, his white hair flew behind him, and still the oaths came. By the time he reached the first floor the room had cleared and there was not a sign of a boy. Dan slowly climbed the stairs muttering to himself while the boys rolled through the hay in the barn with uncontrolled laughter.

The wind rustled the trees, the smell of fresh-picked black walnuts still in their hulls filled the room with a tart smell and the train whistled a mournful low moan as it cut through the prairie towards Hoag. All was quiet except the rain, gentle and steady against the roof. The white beard sunk to the chest and the old fire-eater dozed.

# VII

# Politics and Family
## 1889 – 1902

The late eighties brought reminders of the desert back to Nebraska again. Crops were short, prices high, and debts neck deep. There was a clamoring for a change in the tax system and a deflated dollar. The need for farmers to organize became imminent. Farmer's Alliance locals sprang up so rapidly the charter numbers had to take a first come first served place among charter applications. The Farmer's Alliance soon became associated with the people's party, a political party designed to serve the people. Some of the state officials of the Farmers Alliance became alarmed that the militant farmers were assuming too much politics in their organizations. The state sent questionnaires to seek out feelings of all the locals on this matter. To their astonishment the Farmers Alliance in Nebraska answered back, "not enough politics. We must change the inequities at their source—the political parties are not giving us adequate farm programs." They clamored for more politics in their organizations. They rallied, paraded, held public debates, and gave speeches which had never been equalled in the state history.

On February 14, 1890 the Blakely Farmer's Alliance formed in Blakely Township. Its staunchest supporters were Daniel Freeman and his son Samuel. Horace Wickham was elected chairman; J. K. Lewis, vice chairman; Samuel Freeman, secretary; W. D. Rogers, treasurer; A. J. Reedy, chaplain; and Fred Wolf, sergeant at arms. James Heatherington delivered a short and interesting talk along with Sydney Rossiter, E. M. McLaughlin, J. Walker, Frank Wickham, and Sam Rogers. Daniel Freeman delivered the speech and was elected delegate to the next county Alliance to be held February 22, 1890. Sam Rogers was elected alternate delegate. This Blakely Farmers Alliance was later issued charter number 1101.

With the formation of the Farmers Alliance and the Populist Party, Dan Freeman had at last begun to realize his dream of a government for the common man, by the common man. The magnitude of the Farmers' problems and needs were reflected in many of the names they gave their alliance locals: *Equality*, *Independent*, *Hard Scrabble*, *Running Water*, *Prosperity*, *Defense of Home*, *Freedom*, *Cold Point*, *Silver Star*, and *Snow Flake*. It was not unusual for a Farmers Alliance local to operate as a secret organization. They were fearful of political spies infiltrating their meetings, or of strong armed hoodlums who were opposed to the organizations and sought to break them up by force and violence if necessary.

The first populist convention brought cheers, shouts, amens, and thirty four solid minutes of applause at the end of reading the "Pops" platform when it was stated that "wealth belongs to him who creates it." Later in '94 the populist party fused with the Democrats. They were able to elect a congressman, a senator, and a governor through the fused party. Later in 1896 the fusion carried over onto a national scale and the silver tongued orator William Jennings Bryan of Nebraska was nominated for President.

The 1890's again found the farmers moving out of the territory. Crop failure coupled with the depression had broken many backs economically. Danny Hartman lived in the little house opposite the brick house and helped Dan as a hired man.

Slocum Shepard lived south of the homestead. Both families said many times later that they could not have survived the winter without the flour, grain, and turnips Dan gave them. They were not isolated cases of Dan's unstinting generosity. Darius Wells often walked to the homestead and announced to Dan, "I'm 'bleeged to borry some grist fer mill, Dan. The woman's clean outta bread and the youngun's are hungry."

Dan would hesitate for a bit, then grin and say, "I guess I can let you have some. Give me your sack and I'll fill it up."

Wells scraped the ground with his toeless boot, finally looking up. "I'm 'bleeged to borry a sack too, Dan."

That night at prayer meeting, Wells with his self-styled preacher sons-in-law damned the Godless infidel that lived down creek and who only that morning had filled their sacks with grist. They damned, but still they came to that man they knew would never turn them away in their times of need for help, food, or protection.

In April of 1890, Daniel's mother died in Abingdon, only three years after her husband, Samuel. Again Dan made the journey home to help sister Susannah with the burial. He and Sue were all that remained of the Freeman family. Sue wrapped the photo of their parents carefully in paper for Daniel. The soft hazy shroud depicting the spirit between them in the portrait taken for the purpose of eliciting the effect of the belief in Spiritualism that they toyed with—half believing, half dis-believing. The somber Daniel came home again, bitten by grief seeking and needing answers no one could give him.

Early the next year Sam took Olive Benjamin for a wife. They lived with Dan and Agnes in the brick house a couple of years until Sam could build a home on the quarter section that Dan gave them southwest of Ellis. Jim had taken his wife and baby to live in Beatrice shortly after Eliza and Webster Carre were married. He remained there only a short time before going to Lincoln to school.

Just as LeClaire filled the void left by Eliza's marriage, so did Agnes May, born September 4, of 1889, fill that left by Sam and his marriage. Agnes, the youngest child born to Dan and Agnes soon came to be called "Sis."

Dan had the old flintlock muzzle loading gun his great-grandfather Elkana Freeman took from the British in the Revolutionary war when he was a Green Mountain Boy in Vermont. It was the custom in the family for Dan and the youngest son to load the flintlock with powder and paper wads the night before the fourth of July and early the next morning, never later than five o'clock, take it outside and usher in the 4th by firing the bucking, noisy gun. The honor fell to Lee as soon as he was able to hold the gun upright on its stock for his father to load. At least part of the day would be spent in town visiting old timers in the park and eating the picnic lunch Agnes prepared the day before. Properly lunched, the rest of the day was spent listening to fourth of July oratory on the bandstands, and visiting some more.

Dan received a letter from Des Moines. His second son, Charles, was writing to tell him of the death of his brother, Gerald. Dan laid the letter down and left the house without a word. The first son of the first marriage dead after thirty-nine years. He had not known where they were or how they found him. Possibly through Etty? He was torn between going to the funeral, confronting the old hurts, and wiping it again from his mind. He brooded again—mute, pre-occupied. Agnes understood. She left him to his thoughts and to do what he thought was right. The next morning he packed the buggy and drove off without a word.

Martin Rich and Etty were at the funeral. Rich swore he saw Dan at the funeral, aloof and outside at the edge of the crowd. At the cemetery, the rumor gathered momentum again. Dan Freeman was there, but at the edge, in the background—at the edge, they said. Only Rich could swear it. No one else. Charles Freeman bitterly denounced the rumor. How could his father be there and not make himself known or come up and speak to him? It could not be, Charles said. It must not be.

The buggy returned to the homestead. Who could say whether it had gone East, South, West, North, or to Des Moines? Who could say whether Dan had viewed the funeral of his son from the yard and the edge or whether he had simply "hyad" the team across the prairie letting the winds and the distance salve his wounds? Who knew or would ever know? Slowly the man came back to himself and the fiery spirit, temporarily subdued, flourished again, though never quite so powerfully.

He was very fond of daughter Eliza. He often went to see Dade, taking his own favorite lunch of jerky, sardines, and crackers. When Ed and Mabel Carre asked their grand-dad what he was eating, he'd reply loudly, "Mule meat," and laugh uproariously. "Ever eat mule meat before? Here, have some." At the offer, they would run away giggling and hide for fear he'd make them eat the unpalatable looking stuff.

Still burning under the beating of his predecessors, Isaac Frantz, Gage county treasurer sold lots 7, 8, 9, 10, 11, 12 of Freeman's subdivision, the former Court House Square, to collect money for assessment of curbing and sidewalk tax. In a suit, Freeman vs. Frantz, treasurer of Gage County Nebraska Freeman declared the sale of this property to be illegal for the following reasons: 1) It was not offered at public auction; 2) no return of the lots sold was filed; 3) said land was not advertised for sale for said taxes and assessments; 4) City Council did not valuate the property before sale, thus acted illegally; 5) no public notice by City Council; 6) law requiring paving had not gone into effect at time council acted and sold the land; 7) Court Street only was to be paved; 8) Court Street pavement was not even an absolute order; 9) after the order was given, Court Street was paved in a different and inferior manner than that filed in the petition to pave it; 10) majority of owners, including Freeman, had been illegally assessed.

Freeman received an injunction and the case was

dropped. Frantz had hoped to become a hero by doing what his predecessor Hiram Webb had failed to do. The right and wrong of the long standing squabble was not even remotely considered by the city officials. They were either too involved with other problems or too concerned with the requests of other citizens to judge the morality of the Freeman claim. Frantz was the last public official careless enough to bring the case up.

More privately, isolated incidents erupted like the one with old man Holliday who either sought to curry favor with Dan's enemies or who simply wanted justification for his behavior when he drove out to the homestead in the dead of night, pulled up to the barn, and loaded a set of harness, several bushels of corn, and some buckets onto his buck board. When Frank surprised him in the act, demanding to know what he was doing, Holliday answered, "The Lord sent me to get my own."

"If the Lord sent you to get your own then get your own, not Dan Freeman's. Take that stuff off that buck board and get the hell out of here before I fill you with lead." Frank was furious. He watched as Holliday replaced the articles and as he finished he told him, "If you aren't out of range by the time it takes me to get to the house and get my gun, then it's just too damned bad."

The man was onto the buck board and rattling up the road before Frank could get out of the barn lot. He told his father of the incident next morning and, as was Dan's way most of the time, he did not press charges, but simply dropped the incident with a few cuss words.

Dan went into Beatrice that afternoon and sought out his good friend Volney Whittemore, telling him of the night visitor. Volney was provoked and disgusted. "He just come out and took your stuff cause he figured ever' body'd support him and he'd get by with it. I'd go to the law Dan'l. Hell, you're Justice of the Peace, you ought to prosecute."

Dan shook his head slowly. "If I took time to fight every no account that pulls a dirty trick, I'd never get through and I'd never get anything done of my own."

"Yeah. Like old man Wells saying his herd of cows belong to his old maid sisters to get out of paying taxes."

Dan nodded, sober.

"You take too much off people, Dan'l. Why you always let Wells have grist? Nobody else would."

"I don't judge. I don't bother any man that doesn't bother me."

"You're a helluva good fellow, Dan'l, but sometimes I don't figure you."

Dan withdrew his hand from inside his boot, looked squarely at Volney, and began to laugh. "Damnit-to-hell, the Lord sent me to get my own," he quoted Holliday, and both erupted with good natured laughter that closed the disagreeable subject, and Dan got up to unhitch his mare and ride home. He had just finished hanging the harness when Hiram Odell entered the barn in a flutter of excitement.

"Dan, I was just comin' down the road towards home and seen this whole brood of wild turkeys squatted on the bridge rail jist starin' into Cub Creek. I ain't got a gun with me, could you loan me your musket and by God we'll have roast turkey fer supper."

Dan quickly reached into his spring wagon and withdrew his loaded musket and handed it to Hiram. Hiram flitted from tree to tree keeping out of sight of the flock of turkeys perched along the bridge. He drew up close to the east end of the bridge, aimed at its length, and fired. There was a flurry of wings, wild squawks, and a cloud of feathers. Dan came up as Hiram waded from the creek with the last bird under his arm. They laid the birds out across the bridge to count them.

"I'll be damned, you got seven with one shot." Dan stared amazed.

"Oh, hell, I couldn't of." Hiram was still stunned from the sight of all the birds. But a third count tallied seven. Dan took his musket and the turkey Hiram offered him. It would make a great meal for the big Odell family and a greater story in town next day.

John, grown tall, lanky, and twenty, announced he was going back to Illinois to find work. "Shorty" or "Shorty John" as the family called him had a hankering to earn some money on his own and get away from all the girls beginning to accumulate around the Freeman household. "Shorty can't stand girls," they teased, so he gangled off to Illinois for two or three years to get away from the teasing. He returned, much to everyone's surprise, married to Irene Townsend.

Agnes was very impressed with John's Illinois Irene. She said smugly, "Maybe she'll open some of their eyes around here." As the newness of Irene began to wear off, she became more familiar with John's family. She came to be known as "Irene our eye opener," by the rest of the family and impudently snickered about on occasion.

As Agnes grew older she displayed some favoritism among the children and grandchildren. After Sis was born, she became antogonistic toward Dan in the matter of rearing and disciplining.

Sis wasn't to wash dishers or she'd ruin her hands for piano playing.

Frank soon brought Goldie Benjamin home and presented his parents with another Irish daughter-in-law. Goldie was a younger sister of Sam's Olive. Everytime Dan became angry with his boys and stomped from the house, he flung over his shoulder, "The devil owed me a debt and paid me in Irish daughters-in-law."

Dan celebrated his seventieth birthday in 1896 by planting one thousand new fruit trees in his already large orchard. He replaced the dead and dying trees every year or two for as long as he was on the homestead, and quipped to a neighbor that day, "Why shouldn't I do the same damn thing for the next seventy years?"

He hired Cliff Quackenbush to farm for him this year, the same year Jim came home. The panic of the nineties had reduced jobs and wages for everyone. Sam and Olive took Gladys and moved onto the quarter section near Ellis. In spite of hard money, Frank and Jim pooled their resources, aided by a generous gift from their mother, and bought a fancy new rubber-tired buggy. Saturday afternoon was rainy and muddy and the boys were chafing to get to town. They didn't want to get their new buggy muddy so they hitched a team to Dan's and drove in. Shortly, Dan came out to hitch up his rig and found his buggy gone. "Where the hell's my goddamned buggy?" he thundered.

Cliff explained that Frank and Jim had taken it to town. "They didn't want to get their new buggy muddy."

"Didn't want it muddied, eh? Well, I'll be goddamned. Hitch my team to this damned shiney piece of rubber-tired junk and hurry up." He indicated the boys' buggy.

When Cliff threw the lines, Dan jumped into the leather upholstered buggy with soggy wet boots, and cracked the whip across the horses' rumps. He was so furious, red lines crept over his cheeks above the wild white beard. Cursing he tore out of the yard in the rubber-tired buggy, team running and mud flying. He skidded onto the main road, the buggy slithering from side-to-side on its rubber tires, with chunks of mud flying high into the air. He ran the team clear into Beatrice before he could cool down enough to bring them to a walk.

As Dan grew older everyone in the family became afraid of his occasional stomping fits except Goldie. She was the only one who would brave the storm and stay in the house when he got mad. One such occasion began in the house, flared for about an hour at no one in particular. Finally he removed himself from the house, cursed all the way to the barn and continued a general fire of oaths in the barn.

Agnes put her shawl on and went to the barn where he was cursing the harness he was trying to mend. "Pa, it's time you quieted down," she said gently.

"Pa" just stared at her for a long moment and quieted right down. She could usually manage him, but she knew when the moment was ripe to do it and when it was catastrophic to try. Fortunately, these episodes of temper were rare.

The winter Lee was thirteen he went to the barn one day to find his Pa putting hay, straw, and blankets in the covered wagon. In the front he'd loaded feed for the two Indian ponies. Lee was weak from rheumatic fever and the resultant St. Vitus dance. Thin and pale, he shivered beneath his coat. "What you doin', Pa?"

"Keep quiet."

"Where you goin'?"

Dan gave him a hard look. "Keep still, damnit."

Lee turned to go back to the house.

"You stay right here, damnit, until I harness this team and finish packing the wagon."

Lee was uncomfortable and bothered that his father would act this way. He'd never seen him this way before.

When Dan was finished he turned to Lee. "Get in the wagon. You're goin' with me."

"I can't go like this." He looked down at his ragged everyday clothes. "Ma'll have a fit if I go away like this."

"Goddamnit, get in the wagon and never mind Ma. Keep your mouth shut, you understand? Now when we drive by the house I don't want you ganderin' this way 'n that. Keep your eyes straight ahead and don't be sayin' a damn thing."

Lee did as his father ordered, but felt terrible to leave his mother without saying goodbye or where he was going. He wished he knew where he was going. He wished he could see his mother. Hot tears stung his eyes as they went onto the main road and beyond calling distance. His father

remained aloof and strangely distant with Lee until they
got beyond Blue Springs. Then he turned to the boy. "Get
those blankets wrapped around you and over your head.
Keep warm. This wind is hellish cold."

The blankets drawn around himself and his father in a
good mood again he asked, "Where we goin', Pa?"

"You're a sick boy. I'm gonna take you to get well."

Lee brightened with this prospect but quickly sobered.
"Ma won't know."

"Ma knows we're gone. Time you growed up without
your Ma's apron strings."

At Excelsior Springs in Missouri Dan found a stable for
his team and wagon and took Lee to a hotel.

Lee was put to bed for two weeks, getting up only long
enough to take the hot mineral baths twice a day. Dan
brought to Lee's bed luxurious and different tasting meals
than anything he was used to at home. He'd taken Lee's
clothes, had them laundered and pressed, and stacked them
on the chair beside the bed. Your duds'll be ready when
you are," he smiled.

In two weeks Lee was strong again. He put on the clean
clothes, happy and wondering at this new world he'd never
seen before. Dan drove to St. Joseph to the railroad
station, bought a ticket to Beatrice, put the boy on the
train, and without a word of explanation took off alone in
his wagon. He was untroubled as to whether the boy would
get home safely. When Lee arrived in Beatrice, he hitched a
ride home with old man Reed who lived beyond the
homestead.

When he walked into the house his mother stood looking
at him; no recriminations, no questions. All she said was,
"Why did you go away from home in clothes like that?"

"Pa said they was fine."

"Your Pa would."

"He got 'em washed for me. They was clean, honest."

She walked to him and felt his forehead for fever.

Satisfied that the boy was well, her face relaxed. She shook her head slightly and built the fire up to boil the potatoes. The matter was never broached again.

Dan came home about six weeks later driving twenty head of cattle and leading two new horses. He gave the first dog he'd acquired to Lee. There were no explanations, no questions. That he had been doctoring again was obvious. Galveston? Houston? Perhaps Mobile. But it was somewhere where the sun could warm his aching joints and ease the tightness in his chest.

Late in the same afternoon Mattie Collett rapped on the door, breathless and red faced from pulling her heavy body up and down the creek bank to make the crossing. She drew out a small envelope from her apron pocket and handed it to Agnes. "Read me a letter," she asked.

Agnes took the letter and sat in the rocker and read to the illiterate Mattie. It was a letter from her people back in Ohio.

Mattie rose to go but lingered on her way to the door. Finally, she turned and with an embarrassed shrug of her shoulders asked, "Mrs. Freeman, write me a letter?"

With Agnes' nod Mattie settled down comfortably in the chair again; thinking of bits and scraps of news to have Agnes include in the letter to her folks. Finally satisfied she'd forgotten nothing, she took the sheet of neat script Agnes had written for her, folded it carefully, and dropped it in her apron pocket. "I be back when another one come, Mrs. Freeman?"

Agnes nodded, answering the woman she would again "read a letter to", as she had done many times before and would end up "writing me a letter" as she always did after the letters had been read.

When Lee and Sis walked home from school singing a new song they'd learned, "John Brown's body lies a mould'ring in the grave, John Brown's body lies a m . . ." that was as far as they got before Agnes came in and

cracked Lee across the behind. "I don't ever want that sung
in my house, do you understand?" she said severely.

They didn't understand until much later when Eliza
confided that John Brown was a half great uncle to Agnes
through the Wrights, and if they knew when they were well
off they'd forget they ever knew this. They most certainly
were never to mention to their mother that she'd told
them.

In 1899 Edith Beecher was hired to teach District 21
known as the Freeman school by John Scheve, Henry
Odell, and Matilda Collett, members of the district school
board Gage County Nebraska. At this time, Lee and Sis
were both students in the school. Miss Beecher set about
from the first day of school to read portions from the
Bible, to sing various hymns, primarily pentecostal, and to
indulge in prayers. She asked the students to participate
with her in them during the school hours set aside for
public instruction.

Dan went to the school board and asked that she be
restrained from reading the Bible, praying, and singing
hymns during the school time. They refused to curtail her
religious activity in any way.

He asked the board of education on three separate
occasions for this restriction and was ignored and refused
each time. He then went to L. W. Colby to take the case to
District Court to have the religious practices stopped. Colby
refused, even though he agreed it should be done, because
he was afraid it would cost him his law practice. He then
went to Judge L. M. Pemberton. Pemberton said, "I'll take
it, Dan, if you'll give me twenty-five dollars down. You can
pay me the rest when we're through, but right now I'm
hard up as hell and I need money. But, Dan, you're going
to raise a hell of a row all over the country."

"That's just exactly what I want to do. It's the principle
of the thing and I'm opposed as all hell to it." The petition
of complaint was drawn up on the 31st day of October

1899, and an answer to the petition by the school board and teacher as defendents was given after the writ of mandamus was issued. Defendents answer denied the allegations of the relator and asked that the writ of mandamus be discharged and costs of the action be taxed to the relator. Freeman filed a motion for a new trial and the case was taken to the district court. The decision rendered in the district court was in favor of the defendents—the board of education and the school teacher. Whereupon Freeman took it to the State Supreme Court of Nebraska. The decision of the district court was reversed in Freeman's favor by the Supreme Court in 1902 and the allegations and cross allegations are contained in briefs secured from the Nebraska Supreme Court Reports, September term, 1902, pages 857-873 from Volume 65. (See Appendix B).

Some interesting side lights not specifically contained in the abbreviated Supreme Court Case inserted in Nebraska Reports, Volume 65, were testimonies of the defendents and Freeman. From records of testimony Miss Edith Beecher testified that anything taught in her church was all right to teach in school. Asked if she felt her church encompassed the feelings generally of all religions she answered, "Yes." When handed a Douai version of the Bible and asked if she felt it would be permissible to teach from this book she hesitated then answered, "I suppose it would." Would she read the apocrypha from the Douai Bible in school? She could not answer. She was then informed it was a Catholic Bible, whereupon she raised her hands in protest and said, "Oh, no, no. I could not in good conscious teach from it."

In cross examination Freeman denied he believed in "no" religion. Only the religion of Miss Beecher and the fundamentalist views of her particular kind of church were objectionable to him. He said he "favored no church but leaned somewhat towards spiritualism, and the divine power of the common man." Asked if he was a religious man, he

answered "No." Asked if he had ever attended church, he
answered, "hundreds of times." Asked if he had a church
preference when he did attend, he said "I do not." Asked
if his family attended church, he answered, "They always
go with me."

Dan was raised a Campbellite Christian, but saw fallacies
in religion and in his own religious experiences that made
him doubt and withdraw from it. He attended the services
of probably every different sect known including the
Christian Scientist.

He leaned towards spiritualism because it was a continu-
ation of the Protestant Reformation—a liberalization of
organized religion. It was a withdrawal from the church
begun by his parents as a result of the many deaths of their
children and of the unnecessary deaths imposed upon other
children through the church by means of baptisms and
extreme cruelty by fanatically religious parents. Kindness to
children in a day when strictness and obedience were
foremost among people's beliefs was indeed a deviation
from the convention patterns of human behavior. Beginning
long before the advent of Daniel Freeman, the Freeman
family was long on kindness and short on puritanical
rigidity, as was the Suiter family as well. Dan believed in
the same principles his parents espoused and were famous
for in New England. "Do unto others as you would have
them do unto you." Organized religion and the fraud
contained within it blocked the man from accepting it on
that basis. He put much thought to religion and long hours
were spent in discussion of religion with Judge Colby. He
spent far more time on religion than his counterparts who
professed it, but he seemed to find nothing convincing or
satisfying in it. "The greatest deterrent to his acceptance of
organized religion," Agnes recalled after his death, "was the
vicious, deceitful, and crooked ways in which the pro-
ponents of religion behaved." She cited the illegal moving
and selling of their home, the thousand bushels of grain

stolen from Dan over the Court House Square case, and the uncharitable behavior toward Dan on the part of people who were not even primarily involved. She cited the attempt upon his life after the religion case when someone came to their home in the middle of the night and tried to break a window and enter the house. Had it not been for the hounds and Dan's quick wits to immediately start shooting into the air to frighten them off, the entire family might have been murdered. "He didn't feel that people who did things like that were religious or if they were then he wanted no part of such a religion. When Daniel picked up the pistol the marauder had dropped in his flight, the only thing he said was 'some Christianity'."

It was impossible for Dan Freeman to accept a weak substitute for what he felt should be strong and real. It was mentioned in the court case on religion in schools that Dan may have been unreasonable, but that it was his right as a citizen to be unreasonable. It is interesting to note that most of the progress made by the human race has been made by people who seemed unreasonable at the time and were almost invariably persecuted for their seeming un-reasonableness. Their persecutors often bore the stamp of religious fanatic. Even so, the Jesus Christ so fervently believed in today was also a victim of persecution at one time. Each new generation of fanatics obliterates the trail of destruction of their predecessors and deceives themselves into believing they are the Messiahs of the new generation. Ralph Waldo Emerson said in his *Essay on Compensation:*

> The history of persecutions is a history of endeavors to cheat nature, to make water run uphill, to twist a rope of sand. It makes no difference whether the actors be many or one, a tyrant or a mob. The mob is man voluntarily descending to the nature of the beast. Its fit hour of activity is night. Its actions are insane, like its whole constitution. It persecutes a principle; it

would whip a right; it would tar and feather
justice, by inflicting fire and outrage on the
houses and persons of those who have these.

Defendent's attorney Kretsinger stepped from his role of
attorney many times. He became too emotionally and
personally involved in the case to be of real value in the
defendent's defense. He stepped from his role to denounce
Freeman as a heretic and infidel; passing judgement without
basis, name calling and creating a public atmosphere of hate
in the community. His prejudicial role led him to remark,
the Bible should be read in school as a matter of good
literature, and without question the King James version is
the best example of good literature. Best for which religious sect, he was careful not to divulge. He also stated
the best place to obtain moral training was from the Bible,
therefore, it should be used in school. If significance was to
be attached to this remark then he failed to establish the
need for duplicity by sectarian churches or for parental
morality and training in the homes. He further stated that
no one in the district had objected to the Bible teaching in
the school except Dan Freeman. Freeman stated there were
at least seven Catholic persons who had come to him
privately objecting to the teaching. They were afraid to
protest publicly and help him out. Considering the harsh,
cruel, and so-called Christian treatment dealt to Dan over
the case, their reluctance was understandable. When a
fearless man like L. W. Colby was too frightened to take
the case, one cannot condemn the meek protestor already
prostrated by reason of his minority position.

Doc Wells asked Dan later why he took up the cudgel
for the Catholics since he himself was not one. Dan told
him, "because, goddamnit, religion is a private matter like
who you go to bed with. If I don't want to air mine or if I
haven't got any to air, it's still nobody's goddamned
business."

Asked if he was ever thanked by the Catholics for his

influence in separating church and state in Nebraska, Dan
remarked, "Hell yes. But as soon as they told me, they
slunk off like goddamned beaten hounds and talked about
the goddamned infidel that did incantations by moonlight
on Cub Creek." He laughed heartily. "I don't want anybody's damned thanks. I did what had to be done."
Pointing to Bimfock, Tanny's grandchild, he said, "People
are just like that damn dog. They just wag and lick, and
make over ever' son-of-a-bitch that comes along. Their tripe
don't mean nothin'. The only difference is the damn dog
knows this, but the human is too damn dumb to know it."

It was remarked to one of Dan's descendants by someone in Beatrice, "Dan Freeman never cared what anybody
thought." It was meant to be complimentary, but the sayer
was over-solicitous and lacked insight. Dan Freeman did
care and his family cared, but they had to do what they
felt was right and that took a special kind of courage not
readily understood by the weak.

"When they have to pay the court costs then it'll sink in
their heads they've lost the case," Sam told his father.
"When money is involved it means more to them."

"I'm not concerned with their feelings." Dan was tired,
seventy seven, and proud he'd won the main victory. "I
wasn't trying to fight these people—only a principle of
right."

When Scheve learned that the board had to pay the
court costs, he began to complain about never having really
wanted to fight the thing in the beginning and blamed the
teacher for backing the board into an uncomfortable position, saying "she come to our school with that idee in
mind right from the beginning." But the school board paid
for the litigations, nevertheless.

Feelings had reached such a pitch that when Clara
Frolick came to teach in the Freeman school in 1902 she
was ordered by the school board to conduct whatever
religious exercises in the school she desired. She had always

sufficed with the reading of the Lord's prayer and felt
more than a verse or two in addition to this was excessive.
On once occasion, she finished reading the Lord's prayer to
her pupils and looked up to see a giant of a man with a
bushy sprawly unruly white beard lathered across his face
that met up with the flowing white hair, standing in the
hallway at the entrance of the room. She was visibly
shaken when she recognized the blazing eyes as Dan
Freeman's. Except for the movement of his beckoning
finger he was motionless.

She walked up to him fearfully, frantically fighting the
thoughts in her mind that this would end her teaching
career and she would be fired. She stopped in front of the
tall lean man and before she could speak his hand reached
out and rested upon her shoulder. "You did fine," he said.
"Not overdone and pushing it down the students' throats.
You did fine." He patted the shoulder his hand touched
and before Miss Frolick could utter a word, an animated
shadow flicked across the wall through the doorway and
Dan was gone as silently as he had come.

He never came back again, but he was so nice
about it I could have cried. He was nothing like
what they'd said. Later the same year as I was
getting over the small pox, Mrs. Freeman, who
was on the school board at the time, came to see
me and to examine me to see if I could come
back to school without spreading the disease to
the pupils. She was so nice to me and polite and
so very dignified.

# VIII

# The Waning Years
## 1903 — 1909

In the midst of the suit to separate church and state Dan's sister Sue died. Agnes and Dan both went east leaving their children home. They never subjected their children to funerals and attended as few as they could themselves. Agnes called funerals "sick orgies, appealing to the morbid in people." The eastern visit was brief because of the pending court case that Agnes had never wanted Dan to pursue in the first place. Not because she was in disagreement, but because she "knew how mean people could be."

When Galusha Grow retired from congress in 1903 the town of Montrose in Pennsylvania planned a homecoming for the "father of the homestead act." As part of the festivities Dan was asked to be there, acting as the first homesteader in the U.S. Dan accepted the invitation and Agnes immediately insisted he buy a new suit for the occasion. Though he saw little need for one he placated his wife and bought a black cavalry twill edged on the lapels, front, and cuffs with black satin in the latest style. He boxed the new suit neatly and carried it along for a fresh change, wearing his old suit on the trip. When he arrived, he was greeted at the station by Grow, taken to the Courthouse steps to review the parade, and finally driven to the Fair Grounds for the special addresses, songs, and pomp and ceremony. Dan spoke with his usual oratorical rhetoric briefly describing his filing on the first homestead and pressing elaborate praise onto Congressman Grow. The ceremony concluded, Dan boarded a train for Beatrice with an armload of newspapers and pictures of the event. There were pictures with Freeman and Grow at the depot, Freeman and Grow in the reviewing section on the Courthouse steps, Freeman and Grow on the speaker's platform at the Fair Grounds, Freeman at the rostrum, and Freeman and Grow waving good-bye to the crowd. "But there's not one picture of Freeman in his new suit," Agnes moaned with mortification.

It seems likely that the homecoming of Galusha A. Grow and his acceptance of Daniel Freeman as first homesteader set the precedent for the national acceptance of his number one position. Grow's acceptance was based strictly upon the record books in the U.S. Land Office where Freeman's claim was and is designated application no. 1, entry no. 1, proof of residence number one, patent no. 1, recorded on page one of book one.

After Dan returned from Montrose, he hitched up his spotted pony team to the buggy and drove to Beatrice. "Say Uncle Dan, I ain't seen you for a spell. I heard you had one foot in the grave," Old Man Stevens remarked.

Dan began dancing a jig in the street, stopped and answered, "Which foot?" They both laughed hilariously. He then proceeded in to see Doc Wells.

At the turn of the century Dan, Agnes, Sis, and Lee went to Kentucky to visit Agnes' cousins the McBrayers. The McBrayers were wealthy distiller-landowners and some of the older members were southern sympathizers. James McBrayer who lived in Lawrenceburg, Kentucky met the Freemans at the train. After spending an enjoyable time with Jim's family, they visited Louis, then William McBrayer, and finally James' son Lucian. Lucian had a young son James, who taught country school while his spinster sister Mattie oversaw Aunt Sue, a Negro housekeeper who lived with them. The Freemans were hospitably entertained among the cousins with the proverbial and famous southern hospitality. Agnes' cousins treated Dan like royalty. He was greatly respected and admired by them. Towards the end of their stay, they were to be entertained in the home of Louis McBrayer's son. They were to stop for Louis and bring him along. When they stopped at Louis McBrayer's house, they found him too drunk to descend the steep path to the waiting carriage. He stumbled and slid the rest of the way on his behind. When he got up to climb into the carriage, his whisky bottle fell out of his pocket and struck the rim of the carriage wheel and broke. As soon as he dismounted at his son's house he asked his daughter-in-law, "play Dixie for me, Sophia, then I'll go home."

She promptly complied by rendering a quick and spirited version of Dixie on the piano. When she finished, he rose and with a final sour anesthetized stare at the Freemans, turned and walked home much to the relief of everyone present. Obviously entertaining yankees did not agree with him.

While Agnes found the incident tense and unnerving, Dan was greatly amused and entertained by cousin Louie's anti-Yankee feelings.

It was the last big trip the Freeman's would make together. Dan used his cane more, found entertainment among his pioneer cronies in town, and nursed his aching joints.

When the telephone came to the homestead, the offspring were enamored with the device. Their granddad deplored the "contraption" and objected to its being brought into his home. The Irish daughter-in-law won out and the phone was installed in both her and Frank's frame house and the old brick house a few hundred feet away. Dan was slowing down some and losing his hearing. Goldie called the brick house soon after the phones were installed. Being the only one in the house, Dan was forced to answer.

"Hello, grandad?" Goldie shouted. "Can you hear me, Granddad? Can you hear what I say?"

There was a long pause then a spirited quip, "No,

damnit. I can't hear a damn word you say," and hung up abruptly.

The exchange prompted Goldie to say afterward when someone solicitously remarked perhaps Dan hadn't heard, "He hears what he wants to hear."

William Jennings Bryan delivered his "The Victories of Peace" address in Beatrice in 1907. In it he said,

> The homestead act was instrumental in bringing about a peaceful conquest of the desert west. It offered an inducement, a reward for the settlement and the result is that the desert has been made to blossom as a rose. The pioneers endured hardships and made their homes on the lonely prairie. They were men and women who gave the world more than they took from it.
>
> The first one to take advantage of the homestead act was a Freeman, and the name is a good one, for the law was framed to make free men and a free people.

At this point Bryan's attention was brought to the presence of Daniel Freeman standing as close to the speaker's platform as he could press, both to hear and to see the man he'd admired so long. Bryan turned and warmly shook the hand of the venerable pioneer.

That winter Dan and Agnes went to Sulphur Springs, Arkansas where Dan doctored his rheumatic joints in the mineral baths and rested his heavy chest under the warm winter sun. It was there he slipped and fractured his hip. Wanting to be home, he disregarded the fracture and insisted on making the train ride back to Beatrice. He was a pioneer wasn't he? He'd gone through much worse than this before on the frontier where the saddle was the only pillow a man had? Grim and pale, he withstood the ride back home to his homestead, the claim, the only home he accepted. Healing was slow and his hacking cough persisted and magnified. They must move into the Freeman property

on 1000 Lincoln Street where Doc Gass could keep vigil.
Agnes took her Daniel into town where she hoped intensified treatment might help him.

The papers were spread about him. They were carfully
rolled and burned and fresh ones laid. Still the hacking
persisted and intensified. Months of coughing and agonizing
pain.

He called to Agnes. "It's a strange thing," he told her
haltingly. "I keep seeing Uncle Sammy Kilpatrick. Sometimes it's Nathan Blakely. Once ol' Joe Graff. The people
we knew when we came here. Then again they're gone.
They tell me something—a new land and peace." He dozed
peacefully. He woke again and asked of Agnes, "put me on
the east hilltop so I can watch over my homestead and my
boys."

> The wind, the wind rushes past my ears and
> tickles my whiskers. Round the bend and over
> the rise an' I'll win this race. Why, damnit it's
> 'cause your horse ain't fast enough. Hell man,
> you want a fast mare don't trade with no bush-
> whacker. Sure, I see ol' Sammy and Joe Graff
> too, thrashin' like hell in that poison ivy. What
> the hell's Job Harris a' doin' out on my claim?
> Come on, now, git—git back there and take your
> fill a that O-hi-ee apple butter 'fore the damn
> stuff's gone. Hey you, Wib and Wash Rogers
> don't just stand there cluckin'. Get the hell on
> an' round your women folk up, lyceum's at our
> house tonight. Aggie baked apple pies outta
> Nebrasky apples, beats the hell outta O-hi-ee
> butter. I see the prairie schooners and the carts
> draggin' them poor ol' milk cow critters behind. I
> see the wheels turning on the rutted trail but the
> sound is fading. Damnit-to-hell, Aggie, I can't
> hear a thing."

As the sound was muted, the visions fused and blurred
and darkness fell—solidly, totally.

One day short of the forty-fifth anniversary of his filing the homestead claim he slumped in the chair like the bold pioneer he was—bravely, quietly, and peacefully. The wild white beard sprawled like the windblown Russian thistle across his chest and the blazing eyes closed forever.

Dan was buried on the brow of his favorite lookout point on his beloved homestead on the north lot, with the G.A.R. conducting the final commitment at the grave.

The inscription on his monument reads:

> Daniel Freeman Born Preble Co. Ohio Apr. 25, 1826 Filed on First Homestead in U.S.A. Jan. 1, 1863 and lived on it until his death Dec. 30, 1908 Soldier, Doctor, Sheriff and Farmer A True Pioneer

General L. W. Colby, long time friend and colleague of Dan's delivered the funeral address. The culmination of a long series of discussions, many upon religion, was at hand. No one knew Dan's philosophy and religious convictions better than Colby. Like Brothers, they had both endured many long delving discourses upon the subject of religion. Both sought answers to man's origins and departures, neither could accept the doctrine of heaven, or of believing blindly and unwittingly the dogma of the churches. Dan wanted to see, to touch, to observe, then he would believe. He would not be a tool blandly accepting what he was told to accept. He was an individualist, a seeker of answers and truth. He was a champion of the poor.

*Speech of Gen. L. W. Colby, Jan. 2, 1909 at the Funeral of Daniel Freeman.*

Comrades and Friends:

Death with dark and heavy hand will come with unfailing certainty and knock at the door of every household in the land, and each person in turn must sooner or later answer the call. When he comes to those with youth and health and hope before them, they shrink from the messenger and the coming is looked upon with dread, and often with terror; but the knock is heard by the infirm, sick and aged generally with acquiesense and often with relief and content. The dread reaper found our old friend waiting after months of sickness and suffering, and at the ripe age of over four score years. Daniel Freeman died at about 6 o'clock on Wednesday evening of December 30, 1908.

It is said that death should seal the lips of unfriendly criticism, but it should also seal them against untruthful eulogies and the fulsome and indiscriminate praise of the departed. Our dead friend despised hypocrisy and falsehood and would not receive undeserved commendation. I shall attempt only a brief sketch of the life and character of the venerable man whom I have personally known for the past thirty-six years and whose acts in war and peace are a part of the history of our great commonwealth.

Daniel Freeman was born in Preble County, Ohio, April 25, 1826, the oldest son of Samuel Freeman of the State of Vermont. When ten years old he moved with his parents to Knox County, Illinois, where they lived to a good old age. At the outbreak of the War of the Great Rebellion he enlisted in the Union Army, being detailed on special service in the west and southwest and served with honor till the close of the war.

While in the military service on January 1, 1863, at Brownville, Nebraska, he made his entry under the Homestead Act which gave him the well known distinction of being the first Homesteader in the United States, of which he was justly proud. At the close of the Civil War in 1865 Mr. Freeman returned to Nebraska and to his homestead five miles west of Beatrice, built his log cabin and made his home on the land that is officially known as the first homestead, being entry No. 1, proof of residence No. 1 patent No. 1, recorded on page 1 of book No. 1 of the General Land Office of the United states at Washington D. C. This quarter section of land has been for nearly forty-six years and was still his home owned by him and free from encumbrance at the time of his decease.

Hon. Galusha Grow, for many years a member of Congress and the author of the Homestead Act, in a speech referring to this law said:

"There are two interesting instances connected with the final passage of the original homestead bill. First, it took effect on the day of Lincoln's emancipation proclamation. Second, the first settler under the homestead bill, which provided free homes for free men, was named Freeman.—The first settler under this law was a Freeman and I trust the last of its beneficiaries in the long coming years of the future will be a free man."

Our deceased comrade had many experiences requiring nerve, endurance and wisdom in the Indian raids which were in the Little Blue River region and the Republican Valley from 1864 to '67, and with his wife and family suffered the privations and hardships incident to pioneer life and border warfare. Mr. Freeman was twice married; first, to Miss Elizabeth Wilber who died in 1861, leaving three children, and second, to Miss Agnes Suiter who with her six children survive him.

Mr. Freeman always took an interest in public affairs of the State and Nation, and until the past few years was an active factor in the building up of Gage County. While not a politician in the ordinary sense, he held offices of trust and responsibility. He was sheriff of this County in the early seventies, and was Justice of the Peace for many years in his home township. As an officer he was competent, faithful and uncorruptable, performing his duties intelligently and without fear or favor. He was not a party man, but always advocated the independence of the voter.

Daniel Freeman was always patriotic and a lover of the fundamental principles of this government; he believed in the liberty and the equal rights of all men under the law without regard to color, race or sex. He fought for the Union and was willing to lay down his life that the nation might live as an embodiment of these principles.

His ideas and opinions on all matters were openly and fearlessly expressed, and his associates knew where he stood on all questions public or private.

Mr. Freeman's views on religious liberty were pronounced, and he stood firmly on the basic idea of the separation of religion and government as a part of our public institutions. This led him to oppose the teaching or the reading of the Bible in our public schools, and to have the question settled by a final adjudication of the Supreme Court of our state. Mr. Freeman was a man of great mental and physical activity, vigor and force; he was courageous and resourceful; he hated his enemies and loved his friends—and told them so; he was never cast down by defeat or exalted by victory.

In religion Mr. Freeman belonged to the class commonly termed freethinkers. He did not accept the doctrine of vicarious atonement, and he believed that the Bible was no more inspired than the good things to be found in other books or religions other than the Christian. He believed in God as the Creator and ruler of all things, and that the soul of man is immortal.

He was an admirer of Robert Ingersoll and held many of the views of the great orator. He claimed man could not know the future life,—but could only believe and hoped he stated that the following paragraph in Ingersoll's address at his brother's grave expressed the extent of human knowledge of our existence:

"Life is a narrow vale between the cold and barren peaks of two eternities. We strive in vain to look beyond the heights. We cry aloud, and the only answer is the echo of our wailing cry. From the voiceless lips of the unreplying dead there comes no word; but in the night of death hope sees a star, and listening love can hear the rustle of a wing."

To him life seemed a ship pursuing an unknown voyage with a nameless pilot sailing a chartless ocean; and yet during the last weeks of his sickness and suffering in peering across the dark, striving to pierce the veil, he thought he saw in the dim beyond Nathan Blakely, Joseph Graff, Uncle Sammy Kilpatrick, and other pioneers of his early years beckoning from the shadowy shore, and the vision brought him comfort and rest.

Our white haired friend of many decades answered the call of the grim messenger fearlessly and hopefully; he died as he had lived with his face to the foe a brave and honest man, and he embarked for the "The undiscovered country from whose bourne no traveler returns," repeating in his spiritual consciousness the last sweet words of the immortal Tennyson:

Sunset and evening star,
And one clear call for me!
And may there be no moaning
    of the bar
When I put out to sea.

But such a tide as moving seems
    asleep,
Too full for sound and foam,
When that which drew from out
    the boundless deep
Turns again home.

Twilight and evening bell,
And after that the dark;
And may there be no sadness of
    farewell
When I embark!

For tho' from out our bourne of
    time and place
The flood may bear me far,
I hope to see my pilot face to face
When I have crossed the bar.

It was his request and it is fitting that these mortal remains should be laid to rest on the land he loved so well and beneath the trees planted by his own hand in the early years of danger, toil and privation.

May the grass grow ever green and the flowers breathe their purest perfume over the grave of our comrade and distinguished pioneer; may the mellow voiced quail, the meadow lark, the brown thrush and the song birds chant their sweetest requiems near the last resting place of him who always loved and protected them from wanton destruction; and when the sacred dust is lowered by faltering comrades back to its mother earth this afternoon may we all remember that it was by such strong hands, brave hearts and indomitable wills as his that the great American desert plains have been made to blossom like a rose, the foundations of our republic have been sustained and cemented, and freedom, human equality, and justice made the guiding principles of this peaceful and prosperous nation under the best government the world ever saw.

## DAN'L FREEMAN DIES

### First Homesteader Passes Away At Home In This City — Close of a Busy Life

One by one the pioneers lay down their burdens of earthly cares and pass to a better world, leaving a memory of works well done and a record of difficult tasks faithfully performed.

Daniel Freeman, the first homesteader, died at his home in this city shortly after 6 o'clock yesterday evening, after an illness of over a year.

Mr. Freeman was one of the best known residents of Gage county, enjoying the distinction of being the first man to file his claim on a homestead in the United States under the homestead act of 1862. The first homestead was Mr. Freeman's home for nearly forty-six years during which time he took active interest and occupied a conspicuous position in the affairs and history of Gage county.

Daniel Freeman was born in Preble county, Ohio, on the 26th day of April, 1826, and at the time of his death was in the eighty-third year of his age. His father, Samuel Freeman, was born in Vermont in the early part of the last century, and was a member of an old New England family. In 1835 Samuel Freeman and his wife moved to Knox county, Illinois, and were among the pioneers of that state.

Mr. Freeman was the second child and the oldest son born to this marriage. His parents both lived to a good old age, and died in the Illinois home. Daniel was ten years of age when his parents moved to Illinois and was in the vigor of manhood at the outbreak of the Civil War. He enlisted in the Union army and was detailed in the west and southwest, and it was while on this special work in Nebraska that he filed upon his homestead, which is located on section 26, in Blakely township of this county, being the first man to take advantage of the government homestead act.

He was married in Illinois to Miss Elizabeth Wilber, who, like, himself, was a native of Ohio and came to Illinois in her youth. She died in 1861, leaving three children. In 1865 he was married in Scott county Iowa to Miss Agnes Suiter, who with her six children, still survive him. Mrs. Freeman is now sixty-five years of age.

The story is that Mr. Freeman's filing upon the first homestead was quite by accident, rather than by design. He was in Brownville late in December, 1862, and, while at the hotel at that place, he attended a social entertainment where he met a young man who had been commissioned as clerk to the receiver of the land office. Mr. Freeman was then on a furlough and under orders to report to headquarters and so had a very short time in which to file his application papers. At a little past midnight on the 1st of January, 1863, he made his entry in the land office and immediately started back to his place in the army. His entry was No. 1, his proof of residence was No. 1, his patent No. 1, recorded on page 1 of book No. 1 of the land office of the United States.

The author of the homestead act was Hon. Galusha Grow. In a speech in congress some years after he said: "There are two interesting instances connected with the final passage of the original homestead bill. First, it took effect on the day of Lincoln's emancipation proclamation, Second, the first settler under the homestead bill, which provided free homes for free men, was named Freeman. The first settler under this law was a Freeman and I trust the last of its beneficiaries in the long coming years of the future will be a free man."

Mr. Freeman was a hardy, rugged man, patriarchal in appearance, and with bright, piercing eyes that never lost their luster until closed in the eternal sleep.

He is survived by his widow and nine children, Mrs. M. A. Rich of Kansas City, Charles Freeman of Des Moines, John Freeman of Lyons, Ia., Mrs. D. W. Carre, Samuel, James, Frank, Lee and Miss Agnes Freeman, all of Beatrice.

As yet no arrangements have been made for the funeral.

*Beatrice Daily Sun*
*Dec. 31, 1908. p. 1, col. 3-4*

## DANIEL FREEMAN PASSES AWAY

### Pioneer Resident Dies at His Home After a Lingering Illness

### WAS THE FIRST HOMESTEADER

### Located on First Homestead Nearly Forty-six Years Ago — Was Well Known Throughout Nebraska

Daniel Freeman, the first homesteader, died at his home in this city, 1000 Lincoln Street, last night shortly after 6 o'clock, after an illness of over a year's duration.

His death was not unexpected, as Mr. Freeman had been in a serious condition for the past week, and had been constantly under the influence of opiates since Sunday evening.

The deceased was in the eighty-third year of his age. He was born in Preble County, O., April 26, 1826. He was a son of Samuel Freeman, who was born in Vermont and who emigrated to Knox county, Ill., in 1835. Daniel Freeman was the second child and the oldest son to this marriage. His parents both lived to an old age and died in Illinois.

Mr. Freeman was well known in Nebraska and throughout the country by reason of the distinction of being the first man to claim on a homestead under the Grow act.

Mr. Freeman was married in Illinois to Miss Elizabeth Wilber, who passed away in 1861. He was again married in 1865 to Miss Agnes Suiter of Scott county, O., who still survives him. Besides his widow he is survived by nine children. They are Mrs. M. A. Rich of Kansas City, Charles Freeman of Des Moines, Ia., John Freeman of Lyons, Ia., Mrs. D. W. Carre, Miss Agnes Freeman, Samuel, James, Frank and Lee Freeman, all of this city.

While south over a year ago Mr. Freeman was taken sick and was confined to a hospital at Sulphur Springs, Ark. For a time his life was despaired of but he recovered sufficiently to be brought to the old homestead in Blakely township west of Beatrice. The latter part of August the family purchased property and removed to Beatrice, leaving the farm in charge of two of Mr. Freeman's sons.

Had Mr. Freeman lived but thirty hours longer it would have been forty-six years since he filed on the first homestead in the United States.

Funeral arrangements have not yet been made but the services will probably be held Saturday afternoon.

### Sketch of Mr. Freeman

When Daniel Freeman filed on the first free homestead provided for free men, at one minute past 12 o'clock on the morning of January 1, 1863, he simultaneously inaugurated the history of homestead entries which has since developed the western prairies into the mecca of American agriculture. On this homestead Mr. Freeman was still living on the quarter section of land for which the first patent was ever issued. He was still in possession of this old patent which he regarded as one of most interesting and valuable relics of American history. Its face indicates that Freeman made entry No. 1, his proof of residence was No. 1, his patent is No. 1, recorded on page No. 1, of Book No. 1, in the United States land office.

Freeman's name is linked with that of Galusha A. Grow of Pennsylvania, once speaker of the lower house of congress, and whose maiden speech in the house was on the subject of "Man's Right to the Soil" That speech was made in 1852, but it was not until ten years later that he was able to see his measure, the homestead law, recorded in the statute books.

### Incidents of Filing

Freeman at that time was a young soldier, detailed on secret service to perform a mission at Brownville, Neb., where the first United States land office was opened. The presence of many prospective settlers awaiting the opening January 1, 1862, of the land office, to take advantage of the homestead law, attracted Freeman to the idea of securing a free home. On December 30, however, he was ordered to report in St. Louis, on a new assignment. To add to his troubles January 1 was a legal holiday. The young soldier, nothing daunted, sought out James Bedford, who had charge of the government land office and told him his troubles. Bedford agreed to sign the filing papers following the stroke of midnight the following night if Freeman could secure the consent of other prospective settlers to waive their right to make entries until the following day. All day December 31st, Freeman sought out the settlers and se-

cured their consent to the scheme, in order that he might get away New Year's morning. There was a dance at the town hall in the evening and at midnight all the young Beau Brummels repaired to the land office to see Uncle Sams hero become the first homesteader. The papers already had been made up and were signed just after 12 o'clock. Freeman started at once for St. Louis and was able to visit the land but twice during the next three years, the law making special provision for soldiers.

### Log Cabin First Structure

In 1865 Freeman laid down his arms and took up the peaceful pursuits of agriculture on his claim. He built a log cabin which was the first structure on the farm. On an adjoining claim lived a young woman with whom Freeman had become acquainted during his previous visits and when the cabin was completed they were married and moved into the new home. Freeman was an energetic fellow and his labors were crowned with success. From an open prairie homestead the quarter section was developed in the finest farm in Gage county. Additional land was purchased and Freeman became wealthy. Three fine orchards surround a fine brick dwelling and a forty acre timber claim had deveoped into a young forest.

Of late years Freeman's health had declined and he had spent considerable of his time at health resorts. He returned recently, however, his health completely shattered.

### Religion and Schools

Daniel Freeman took much interest in politics but never sought office. He was a pioneer Indian fighter and carried two scars as the result of bullets from the Indian's rifles. One of his greatest characteristics was his free thinking. He always maintained that the Bible was made for the people who believed in it, and that they had no right to force it upon persons who did not want it. Taking this stand, he brought the famous lawsuits to force the Bible out of the Nebraska schools. The suit was brought against the school board of his home district.

Freeman ever linked his name with the cause of freedom, and forcefully carried out the policies to be contended for. He took up and fought for the standard raised by Abraham Lincoln. When it came to the question of free homes he was the leader, and his greatest hobby was free homes for free men guided by free thoughts and a clear conscience. He had been successful in carrying out his own system of economics and has never failed to impress his ideas on others when he had the opportunity.

Freeman frequently declared he was ready to die in the cause he had espoused for fifty years.

*The Beatrice Daily Express*
*December 31, 1908, p. 1, col. 1-2*

# IX

# Song of the Prairie
## 1910 — 1932

After Dan's death, Agnes returned to the homestead and the brick house they'd shared since 1876. Frank and John farmed the place with the help of young Clifford Quackenbush. By this time John and Irene had a daughter Evelyn; Frank and Goldie had Daniel, Lila, Dorothy, and Maxine. Samuel and Olive, living near Ellis, had four children, Gladys, Emily, Adelaide, and Samuel Jr. Eliza, living in Beatrice had Grace, Bernice, Mabel, Dean, and Ed.

There were always a number of these grandchildren roaming the homestead, bouncing about chattering with their grandmother. Although Agnes enjoyed her grandchildren's company, there were days and hours when she seemed not to notice them. She often sat and watched the floating branches in the wind among the heavy oak trees of Cub Creek, her thoughts her own, her memories her diet.

In 1909, Sis married Cliff Quackenbush and they lived on the homestead. Agnes continued to oversee and manage the farming. She also enjoyed hitching Fred and Spectre to the buggy and visiting her children. If she drove to Sam's she usually stayed overnight helping Ol in the house or accompanying her grandchildren on their chores. In the summer of 1909 on one of these visits, she went with Adelaide to the field in the buggy to get some sheaves of wheat for Ol's chickens. Adelaide took up the reins and without a word slapped her horse across the rump to start it. Whereupon Agnes said, "You mustn't hit your horse. Speak to it first, then whip it if you must, but always speak to it first. Your pop wouldn't hit you that way. Neither would your grandpa." Her compassion for gentleness and her reverence for Daniel were inseparable to her. Where there was one she would find the other and she would not forget.

For her social activities, Agnes found the Rebeka lodge entertaining and a place she could reminisce with old friends. It helped her to keep contact with things doing in town and among people she and Dan had both known.

When William Griffin was elected mayor of Beatrice in 1911 on the socialist ticket, she followed the proceedings with interest wondering many times what Daniel would have said about the way they got rid of him in two days by quickly adopting a commission form of city government even though he had been democratically elected by the people of Beatrice. "But the Beatrice Sun pawns it off as perfectly legitimate," she scoffed. "How typical of the town and the paper. How typical of people," she told Sam.

"Hitch Merrylegs to the buggy, Dot, we're going to the Diller picnic."

Dot, used to her grandmother's impromptu decisions, ran excitedly to get the horse in anticipation of the excursion.

"I'm cantankerous," Agnes often said. "I'm awful cantankerous just like your grandpa was," and she'd smile happily.

Merrylegs tripped gayly down the road, the little granddaughter eager and happy, the grandmother at peace the best way she knew how to be—traveling, moving behind a horse and feeling the wind against her face the sound of it as it blew past her ears—just as she and Dan would have done it.

The horse was tied to a hitching post in Diller when they arrived and the two drifted into the crowd. When they were ready to go home, Dot went after the horse and buggy only to find Merrylegs had slipped her bridle and was contentedly eating in someone's yard with the buggy drawn up close behind her. Dot quickly drew the bridle onto the horse and galloped down the street, thankful no one had been home. After they'd gone a mile or better

down the road Dot told her grandmother what Merrylegs
had done.

Agnes began to laugh, "You little devil you, git," she
spoke to the horse then tapped her lightly across the rump
with the line.

Agnes enjoyed her buggy rides. She enjoyed her independence of being capable of harnessing her own horse
and hitching it to the buggy. Few women could or would
do this. It was looked upon as being unlady-like to harness
and drive your own rig about alone. Most women would
stay at home and deprive themselves of whatever pleasures
the trip could afford rather than risk their position of
womanliness in public. Agnes deplored such helpless
cringing females. She called them "exploitive leaches," and
in no way could she command any respect for them. She
was infinitely proud of her independence and eternally
grateful to the man who had helped her to achieve it.

On a trip to see her granddaughter, Mable Carre Carpenter in Beatrice one day she drove up in her horse and
buggy, spent the hour, and then trotted down the street
towards home. Mabel's mother-in-law lived across the
street from her and as soon as the dignified, white haired,
old lady had departed in her buggy, the mother-in-law
rushed across the street to demand of Mabel, "Who was
that old peddler pulled up at your place?" Agnes was
capable and a capable woman was to be shunned, looked
down upon by her own exploited and exploitative sex. But
Agnes did not care. She seemed to enjoy shocking the
subordinated members of her sex.

Occasionally Ida Claussen would come out to spend an
afternoon sharing Agnes' porch and reminiscing. After the
brick house burned down, then the cottage with Frank's
Daniel Boyd in it, Agnes lived in the little frame house
scarcely any bigger than the original log cabin that sat on
the homestead in nearly the same spot the cabin had rested
on. It was on the porch of this little house that she rocked

and dreamed and tried to forget the painful memories that
wouldn't stay subdued. It was here she cooked her meals
on the wood range, dusted when the urge moved her,
washed the necessities on the lye-soap scoured wash board,
and threw the potato peelings and dish water to the wind
in the east yard. Here she rocked on the little porch with
old Tom rising occasionally to rub against her ankles and
purr out his pent up affection. A faithful little grandchild
spent much time here with a grandmother who could
shelter and appreciate him. Charley Quackenbush brought
the fuel for the fire, learned to cook the eggs and stew and
to ask the questions that both soothed and irritated that
white haired lady from LeClaire who passed from kitchen
to porch with a limp and a cane.

Charley shared Agnes' Indian stories, the pictures in the
trunk, and her meals. The meals she gladly shared. The
Indian stories—"don't interrupt your grandmother when she
is talking. The trunk—don't touch that. It's a packet of
letters from your grandpa to me. You wouldn't understand
them. That? That's a picture of your grandpa. Funny
looking whiskers? He looked much better than you ever
will, she said irritably. Then more softly, "He wouldn't
have been so good looking without the beard. His mouth
was too straight and wide." She smiled to herself.

Another tintype was shoved too close to her eyes.
"This?" she flustered, became evasive, then lost in thought,
staring at the shifting fluttering cottonwood leaves overhead. At last she drew her attention back to the child. She
took the picture, wiped it across her apron. "This was your
grandpa's brother James. No he's dead. Died in the Civil
War. He was a wonderful man, so young to die." Her voice
was soft and gentle. "I'll show you something if you
promise not to touch again." The child's eagerness coupled
with her own sped her fingers in prying the back from the
picture. "I've never opened this since the day I put it in
here. James cut a lock of his hair before going off to war

and gave it to me to put in here. Don't touch it and don't
talk so much. See? The hair has faded some even being
covered after all these years." She sighed and watched the
leaves flutter again, remembering James, then Daniel. It was
a long time. Things change, age sets in. But the feelings, the
love, they never change. The tear followed the deep crease
across her cheek and dropped onto her lap like a reminder.
She took up the back and carefully drew it into place
across the tintype. That would be enough. It was strange
she'd never opened it before. It wasn't as hard as she had
thought it would be.

"But what about all the rest of the stuff in the trunk,
Grandma?"

"Go play. Scat now." She motioned him away in a
strange voice. Without his question answered or knowing
why, he quickly jumped from the porch and engaged the
old black dog in play.

The wheat in the back of the house swayed in undu-
lating waves with the wind. The cottonwood leaves rustled
above the house. A dog bark in the distance, a boy's call.
The faces blurred in and out with the wheat. Young James.
Daniel's blazing eyes. The white beard like the tumbleweed
that had never tamed. All her babies. Baby Daniel. "I'll
never give up until the highest power in the land says I
must." She dozed until Tom rubbed against her shoe and
stared up at her with a soft questioning meow. "You old
devil, thought I wouldn't wake up to feed you, didn't you?
Charley, Charley," she called. The boy was gone. She
shuffled in to the stove, favoring the hip, but with the
same indominatable air, the same courage that had carried
her through all the homesteading years and the years of
pain before that.

Next day Jim Smith walked out from town looking for
work to help feed his big family of hungry children. Agnes
looked about for some kind of job to give the man. Plenty
to do she supposed. Plenty of able bodied children and

grandchildren to do it. She glanced at Jim waiting expectantly for her answer and then quickly away. Her gaze lighted on the rain barrel by the corner of the house. Why not? It was as good as anything to start on. "I could surely use some help," she beamed having found something at last for him to do. "Fix the drain pipe into the rain barrel more secure and set the barrel up off the ground so it won't rot."

The job was quickly done and Jim knocked on the door. "Done so soon? That was a big job to finish so fast. How much do I owe you?"

Jim, pleased with the praise, answered, "A dollar'll do it, Mrs. Freeman."

"Well, I always inspect the jobs people do for me," she said in mock severity. She went onto the porch, briefly appraised the drain spouts wired securely to the house and the barrel setting off the ground. She turned to Jim, "Oh, you've done much more than a dollar's worth of work. I couldn't possibly take advantage of you that way. She went into the house and emerged with a five dollar bill. "It's worth more but I'll make it up to you another time." She pressed the bill into his hand. "Tell the family hello for me."

Jim looked at the bill with disbelief. "Thank you, Mrs. Freeman, You're a real lady."

If Agnes was tactful in her generosity towards a poor man, she was equally tactful in handling posh businessmen who sometimes came to her to collect bills her sons owed. She graciously turned away one such man who blusteringly demanded the two hundred dollars Shorty John owed him. He was so overcome by remorse for having asked her for her son's bill that he apologized profusely, left without asking John for the money and never pressed for the bill again. "A poor man has to be paid," she'd say, "but it won't hurt a rich man if he never is. Daniel was never harsh about collecting bills owed him, and many's the people owed him and still do."

Agnes began considering parceling her property out to
her children while she was still living so she could enjoy
watching them prosper She was getting on in age and she
had a good many acres to dispose of. She would begin with
the thousand acres in Red Willow County and eventually
end up with the homestead. Her son Samuel objected to
her plan, especially the division of the homestead. "Homestead days are past," she quipped. We don't see Indians
around here anymore, and we don't have huskin' bees.
Folks hurry along to town in motor cars instead of
considering themselves lucky if they were able to jog along
on horseback. Why shouldn't I break up homestead number
one then? It's a relic of a time that is gone."

Still Sam was opposed to her plan. "Think of Pa's part
in it and what he would want." He urged.

"It was hard work to save it and develop it," she
admitted. "I often think every old pioneer could have made
his children comfortable for life if they had worked the
way Daniel did. Daniel was never idle. He never sat still
with time on his hands. He was always figuring on some
way that he could improve our lot and he succeeded. It
seems fit and proper that it be shared now. I think Daniel
would want me to do it this way."

Without further protest, Sam left his mother to carry out
her plan. She began with the Red Willow County land.
Somehow the division that was to begin with the eldest
grandchild belonging to each of her children ran amuck.
She deeded some land to some of them but soon the
urgency of requests by specific children interrupted her
plan and she was forced to reconsider in terms of their
needs.

Dividing the homestead was forgotten temporarily as
Agnes considered her own needs. "I want a place to raise
some chickens, a house to putter about in and make my
own meals. I'll eat what I please," she said angrily. "You

seem to think I'm old," she told her children. "I'm not. I can go to town and see a moving picture show like *Covered Wagon,* the more thrilling the better. I don't need to watch that mush young people think they have to have today." With that, she decided the homestead would remain in one piece and she would continue to supervise it. The next day she ordered Charley to "Pack some duds, you're going back to Iowa with me." She was drained of energy and disturbed by the attempt to settle her property matters amicably.

When the conductor took Agnes' bag and asked her, "Aren't you ever gonna get too old to travel the train?" Charley bristled, but his grandmother ignored the remark. They were six weeks in Iowa where they spent some time in each doting relative's home. They vied for the honor of entertaining their Nebraska relative and her welcome never wore itself out. The sternness left the face of that lady from LeClaire and the frown dissolved during her visit. Charley could tell she was happy.

When they boarded the train for Beatrice it would be her last glimpse of LeClaire. At home, she sat on the back porch quietly watching the shadows playing across the fields on the homestead hillside. She could almost see Daniel up there on the southeast hill pruning fruit trees.

Souvenir hunters pestered her nearly every day hauling bits and pieces and chunks off the old log cabin Dan had built until it was nearly gone. Sometimes they came to the house with their foolish questions. Did she do her own cooking? What did she do with her spare time? Did she smoke or chew? One foolish reporter asked her. "I don't ask you those foolish questions," she told him, "so don't ask them of me. My advice to young people starting out in life today, I'd say three things, don't lie, don't steal, and live within your income. That's putting the matter sort of harshly, but if they live up to those three points in every least bit of a way, I believe they will always be happy."

"Do I want to live in town? What for? Everything I want

is right here. My grandchildren, my little garden, my chickens. O my, yes. I was lonesome at first, but as I got acquainted with my neighbors and accustomed to my surroundings I wouldn't have moved for anything and have never regretted coming here." She had come to the homestead many years ago young, confident. There had been many sorrows, but she still bore the courageous air of indominatable pride and strength that had characterized her whole life and had buoyed the spirit of challenge in her Daniel. Perhaps age had slowed this courageous spirit, but it had not blurred its intensity in the lady who came from LeClaire.

The blurring vision, the unsure step, the hip lamed from rheumatism. She caught her foot in the tangle of the tree root beside her little house. The hip was broken and after a short time she was taken to Doc Fall's sanitorium in Beatrice. It has never been this way it must not be now, she mourned. She begged for her grandchildren and wept for her clothes.

Daniel? How come you to be so slow a comin' after me; Went lookin' for some ol' coon hound, or some fancy steppin' stallion, didn't you? Tanny's right here. Been here all the time right alongside her pups.

Why's it raining like that? Pull over alongside the road and wait it out till morning. Daniel you can't see where your drivin' your horse in this rain. This buggy's snug an' tight, won't leak in to amount to much. Glady's graduation was nice. Wish Diller wasn't so far when we hit an ol' cloudburst like this.

I've missed you Daniel, even the cussin' and frettin'. Why are those grand kids so loud; The catkins are pretty floating along above the Mississippi this way. LeClaire always was the prettiest little town. Was that Ma called me? Pa must be on the wharf. You still here, Daniel? Don't cuss so, soon's the kids bring my duds we'll be gone.

Watch out the window for those pesky Indians. I
never know if they're gonna throw off a hunk of
fresh buffalo meat for you or scalp us. Wish
Lizy'd bring my duds. She knows I can't go
wanderin' the prairie without. Hurry, Lizy. Bring
my black and white check. I've got to find baby
Dan and your Pa's a'waitin' too. Tell Sam and Sis
I'm going' out to the homestead, will you?

She was sedated to forget the hip and to forget her little
house. In a blur of sedation or in a moment of clarified self
preservation she called her daughter to come to her. She
confided in the daughter that a black physic, well known
to the old student of medicine and herbs, had been
administered in a dose that would be lethal in twenty four
hours. True to her word, the next day on the 7th day of
April, 1931, the gaunt white haired lady from LeClaire was
dead at the expressed time.

The depression of the thirties hard upon the family and
the uncertainty of Agnes' state of mind at the time,
prevented the probe. The uncertainty of the event was to
haunt and plague Agnes' daughter to her death, and on to
the daughter she had confided it to.

But of Agnes' eternal sleep, there was no doubt. She
would at last be allowed to go back to her homestead
where she could rest beside her Daniel from the brow of
the east hill. Once again she would take up her patient vigil
beside that gallant man and together they would watch
over their homestead as the meadowlarks warbled the
arrival of a new spring, and the glossy beginnings of new
leaves on the long row of cottonwoods cast their first faint
rustles.

# Appendix A

# Documentation

Who was the nation's first homesteader? Since application papers were not stamped with the hour and minute of filing, it is impossible to determine from existing evidence conclusively who the first homesteader was. However, historical research has narrowed the field down to three main contenders for such a title. Mahlon Gore Vermillion, South Dakota territory, claimed he filed shortly after midnight on January 1, 1863. Gore's claim was lost to a claim jumper and his only connection with the land he filed on was the original file claim. No patent was ever issued to him. William Young, Nebraska City, Nebraska, claimed many years after the January 1, 1863 filing date that he had filed first that he had actually made application December 26, 1862. If this is fact, his claim would not have legally taken affect until 12:00 midnight January 1, 1863—the time Freeman claimed his signature was cast to his application, "upon the stroke of midnight." To further clarify the filing times, or complicate them as the researcher wishes, time zone differentials have entered into the controversy allowing a minute earlier to the Brownville office over the Nebraska City office and allowing several minutes headstart for both Brownville and Nebraska City offices over the Vermillion office. Controversy over who was the real first homesteader has arisen probably more acutely since the establishment of the Homestead Monument.

Since Gore's claim is like the one that got away, can it be said that he ever actually caught it? This seems to narrow the contenders down to two according to the Department of Interior and of the two, one minute might conceivably be conceded to Freeman. While there were more January 1, 1863 claims that extended clear to the Pacific, time zones seem to rule them out as "first" firsts.

John Pethoud and John Adams have each been cited as the first man in Gage county to turn a furrow. Mrs. J. P. Mumford was said to be the first woman to move into Gage County. Which man actually turned the first earth? Can it be proved? And if it can, is it significant? There is really no proof Mrs. Mumford was number one.

Dan Freeman remains on the record books of the General Land Office, of the United States, Washington, D.C. as Entry No. 1, proof of residence No. 1, Patent No. 1, recorded on page one, of book 1.

The Freeman homestead is the site of the Homestead Monument four miles west of Beatrice, Nebraska and whether Freeman was first homesteader by a hair or a hair from being first homesteader seems to be eluding the significance of not only the homestead movement but more importantly to be diluting the importance of the homesteaders and their contributions to the development of a great nation, by getting caught up in super-objectivity which evades the heart of American growth—that is the man, the human element. While it is the considered and carefully weighed opinion of the author after exhaustive and thorough search through files, records, and personal letters that Daniel Freeman is probably the first homesteader in the United States, it is not from this standpoint that he is viewed as a figure of significance.

Rank or prestige can be duly granted in a case that is clearly established, even though its significance is questionable. Enough evidence in the matter of first homesteader is available to grant a "probable" to the recipient. In the case of "second homesteader" which Samuel Kilpatrick has consistently and without challenge claimed

title to, the following facts seem expedient to
relate. Photostatic documentation of land office
records made during the month of January 1863
at Brownville territory, Nebraska have inscribed
the following record, now on file in Washington,
D.C. in the office of Bureau of Land Management
Archives, United States, Department of the
Interior.

January 1, 1863
1st entry, Daniel Freeman, County Gage
2nd entry, Thomas Clyne, County Gage
3rd entry, Phillip Young, County Nemaha

January 2, 1863
4th entry, James B. Robertson, County Pawnee
5th entry, Thomas R. Shannon, County Pawnee
6th entry, David James, County Pawnee
7th entry, George W. Mills, County Pawnee

January 3, 1863
None until 7th of January

January 7, 1863
7th entry, Henry Kramer, County Richard

January 12, 1863
8th entry, John Pittinger, County Pawnee
9th entry, George Cumming, County Pawnee

January 13, 1863
Marks
12th entry, Samuel Kilpatrick, County Gage

January 20, 1863
19th entry, Joseph Graff, County Gage

Samuel Kilpatrick is entered on the 13th day of
January 1863 as the 12th applicant—hardly a
second homesteader. As a matter of newspaper
record Samuel Kilpatrick and Joseph Graff in
later years have stated they were "elbowed" out
on the first day by an aggressive Dan Freeman
who rode with them from Beatrice to the Brownville land office. Freeman had consistently denied
ever knowing either Graff or Kilpatrick prior to

his settling on his homestead in 1865. Since the
books show Kilpatrick the 12th application on
the 13th of January and show Graff the 19th
application on the 20th of January, it seems
noteworthy only to point out the inconsistencies
of these stories perpetrated as truths a hundred
years later.

# *Appendix B*

# Nebraska Reports Reprint

STATE OF NEBRASKA, EX REL. DANIEL FREEMAN, V. JOHN SCHEVE ET AL.*

FILED OCTOBER 9, 1902. No. 11,351.

Commissioner's opinion, Department No. 3.

Religious Exercises in a Public School: BIBLE-READING: SINGING HYMNS: PRAYFR: SECTARIAN DOCTRINE: CONSTITUTION. Exercises by a teacher in a public school in a school building, in school hours, and in the presence of the pupils, consisting of the reading of passages from the Bible, and in the singing of songs and hymns, and offering prayer to the Deity in accordance with the doctrines, beliefs, customs or usages of sectarian churches or religious organizations, is forbidden by the constitution of this state.

ERROR from the district court for Gage county. Tried below before LETTON, J. *Reversed.*

In the year 1899, Miss Edith Beecher was a teacher employed in the public school of district numbered 21, in Gage County, Nebraska. She asked and obtained leave of the school board to have religious exercises in her school. Under the license she prayed, read the Bible and with her scholars sang gospel hymns. This was objected to by Daniel Freeman, a resident of the district, whose children attended the school. The matter was referred to William R. Jackson, state superintendent, for a ruling. He rendered the following decision:

"LINCOLN, NEBR., NOV. 25, 1899.

*"Mr. H. D. Odell, Director, Beatrice, Nebr.*

"DEAR SIR: I am in receipt of your letter of the 23d inst., in which you set forth that a mandamus suit has

*Opinion filed denying motion for rehearing. See page 876.

been instituted against the school board of district No.
21 of Gage county to compel said board to stop the reading of the Bible or singing religious songs.

"In setting forth the conditions and facts in the case,
you show that the plaintiff has heretofore succeeded in
stopping the reading of the Bible, and by so doing has
caused several good teachers to refrain from applying
for your school. You state that nearly all in the district
are in favor of allowing the teacher the privilege of having
her opening exercises, and that you find no one opposed
to it outside of the family of the plaintiff. The exercises
you say consist merely of the teacher's reading from the
Bible and repeating the Lord's prayer, and in a few instances of having singing from the gospel or pentecostal
hymns and offering a prayer of her own composition.
You inquire, 'Am I (considering the above facts) using
good judgment as a member of the school board in refus-
ing to interfere with the teacher's opening exercises?'

"I desire to say in reply that in a district where the
sentiment is unanimously in favor of devotional exercises,
such as reading a chapter from the Bible and repeating
the Lord's prayer, there can be no question as to the right
and propriety of such exercises, especially when the reading of the Bible is without any comment. I do not mean
to say that it would be proper to require pupils to conform to any religious rite or observance, or to go through
with any religious forms or observances inconsistent or
contrary to their religious convictions or conscientious
scruples. Such a requisition would be a violation of the
spirit of the clause in the constitution which prohibits
sectarian instruction. The word 'sectarian,' as defined by
Webster, is 'pertaining to a sect, or to sects; peculiar to a
sect; bigotedly attached to the tenets and interests of a
denomination; as sectarian principles or prejudices.'
Whether or not any particular kind of religious service
at the opening of school work would constitute sectarian
instruction would depend upon the character of the exercises, and would be a question of fact to be determined

State v. Scheve.

in each individual case. As, for instance, a prayer might
be so offered as to be sectarian, but it is not necessarily
so, and in general is not. The same may be said of the
singing. The Bible surely can not be considered as fall-
ing within the category of sectarian books. Indeed, the
Bible is the rarest and richest book in the department of thought and imagination which exists. In its
poetry, its history, its oratory and its logic, it rises into
the solitude of matchless pre-eminence. It is a library
in itself. It has been the inspiration of more literature
than any ten thousand other books put together. The
vitality of Shakspere comes from the moral convictions
of the Bible. It may be pitted against all the books of
all the libraries, out of all races and out of all ages, and
on all the subjects it proposes to handle, and in all the
lines of literature it touches it will discount them all
many fold. Shall pupils be deprived of hearing read in
our schools the book which is the greatest classic of our
literature, the book which touches and crowns all other
branches of knowledge, and is the most widely studied
book in the world to-day? If we were to take the Bible
quotations, direct and indirect, from our literature and
our laws, we would divest them from nearly all that is
high and noble. There is no other book so calculated to
impress on the minds of children and youth the principles of piety and justice and the sacred regard for truth.
There seems to be nothing in the laws of Nebraska that
would prevent the simple reading of the Bible in our
public schools. Judge H. M. Edwards of Scranton, Pa.,
has decided that there is nothing in the laws of Pennsylvania to prevent the reading of the Bible in the public
schools. He says: 'The reading of the Bible in the public schools may be allowed, and even commended, from a
standpoint which does not involve the question of sectarian instruction nor the rights of conscience. It is conceded by men of all creeds that the Bible teaches the
highest morality apart from religious instruction. It
must be admitted that sound morality is one of the

foundations of good character. An education which does not involve the inculcation of moral principles is incomplete. And why can not the common precepts of morality be taught by the reading of the Bible better than in any other way? Furthermore, there is much in the Bible which can not justly be characterized as sectarian. There can be no valid objection to the use of such matter in secular instruction of the pupils. Much of it has great historical and literary value, which may be utilized without violating the constitutional prohibition. It may also be used to inculcate good morals—that is, our duties to each other—which may and ought to be inculcated by the district schools. No more complete code of morals exists than is contained in the New Testament which reaffirms and emphasizes the moral obligations.' Section 4, article 1, of the constitution of Nebraska, recognizes 'religion, morality and knowledge' as 'being essential to good government.' I am, therefore, of the opinion that in this enlightened age and Christian land the public school teacher ought not to be deprived of reading, without written or oral comment, the Bible or of repeating the Lord's prayer.

"Very respectfully,          W. R. JACKSON,
                                    *"State Superintendent."*

Daniel Freeman, sixteen days before the foregoing letter was written, had commenced this action in the district court for Gage county. The decision of the judge at *nisi prius* was to the effect that the matter of text-books, etc., to be used in public schools was to be determined by the school board, and, except in a case of abuse, the court would not attempt to control their discretion.—W. F. B.

*Franklin J. Griffen* and *Richard S. Horton,* for plaintiff in error:

We desire, before quoting the sections of the constitution upon which we rely, to refer generally to the growth of the question now before us. Long before the time of Wyclif, and Luther, the world was dominated by one system of theology. There was one church, and that church

State v. Scheve.

all powerful. After the appearance of Wyclif, Luther and others like them, some of the dogmas of the church were questioned. This resulted in a division of the church into two hostile camps. A struggle began and lasted through the centuries. Honest difference of opinion was not conceded. Whichever party gained the ascendency, attempted to suppress the other with persecution. Nations were involved, wars ensued. In England, the period of the Stuarts, the Commonwealth and Protectorate were distinguished for religious controversy. The English colonies in America were settled by refugees from Europe. Though many of these fled from persecution in Europe, the history of some of the colonies shows a record hardly inferior in zeal to Torquemada or Louis XIV. Roger Williams, the Baptist dissenter, who founded Rhode Island, is well known as one of the few men who questioned the right of the state to interfere with religious conviction. In religious liberty Virginia took the lead. Massachusetts, Connecticut and New Hampshire kept up religious persecution. At the convention called to frame our national constitution were people of variant religious opinions. They could agree on no state religion. The first article of the Bill of Rights—the first ten amendments to the United States constitution—expressly prohibited the national government from exercising such power. Since that time, Madison's maxim, "Religion is not within the purview of human government," has become the settled doctrine in this country. Through a gradual evolution the separation of church and state has finally become established. The result of the growth of religious liberty has been enactments in the different states forbidding the enforced attendance and support of religious worship, and prohibiting sectarian instruction in the public schools. These enactments have not been at the instigation of any sect, or at the demand of any body of persons who did not believe in any religion. They represent the crystallized opinion of Jews, of Catholics, of Protestants, of Agnostics and of various beliefs. These enactments

State v. Scheve.

have become the law of the land, and it is the right of any citizen, whether a believer or unbeliever, to insist upon their enforcement. The reading of the Bible in public schools is simply a relic of the early days which we have outgrown. Any citizen of Nebraska is entitled to invoke the aid of the courts to prevent the violation of the constitution. [Here were cited the parts of the constitution quoted in the opinion of Commissioner AMES.]

The court will take judicial notice of these facts: (1) that the religious world is divided into a large number of sects; (2) that there are material differences between them; (3) that there are Jews, Catholics and Protestants; (4) that the Douai edition (Catholic) of the Bible differs materially from the King-James (Protestant) vers'on; (5) that Catholic and Protestant each have dogmas not believed in by the other; (6) that Protestants are divided into numerous sects; (7) that the Bible of the Jews does not include the New Testament. *State v. Board,* 76 Wis., 177.

It is well to keep in mind that the exercises complained of by the petitioner did not consist simply in reading the King-James version of the Bible, but, also, in offering up prayers and singing religious songs. It will be observed that the facts in the case at bar show more clearly than do the facts in any case hereinafter cited that the exercises complained of constitute sectarian instruction and worship. As stated by Judge Taft,* at *nisi prius,* in *Board of Education v. Minor:* "The singing of Protestant hymns may be used to communicate dogmatic instruction as effectually as the Bible itself. I can not doubt, therefore, that the use of the Bible, with the appropriate singing provided for by the old rule, and as practiced under it, was and is sectarian. It is Protestant worship, and is used as a symbol of Protestant supremacy in the schools, and as such is offensive to Catholics

---

*Alphonso Taft, judge of the superior court of Cincinnati, father of William H. Taft, formerly United States judge of sixth circuit and afterwards commissioner to the Philippines.—W. F. B.

State v. Scheve.

and Jews.  *  *  *  The facts on which this question
turns are simple.  The Roman Catholic denomination has
a different version of the Bible, and includes the
apocrypha as a part of it, which is excluded from the
Protestant Bible.  The Protestant is the King-James
version which the Catholics regard as not only not a
correct translation, but as distorted in the interest of
the Protestant as against the Roman Catholic church.
They object, therefore, on conscientious grounds to having their children read it.  *  *  *  We are not at liberty
to doubt the conscientious objections on the part of the
Catholic parents to placing their children in schools while
the schools are opened by the reading of the Protestant
Bible.  Like the majority of us, the Jews have received
their faith from their ancestors, and according to that
historic faith, the assertion in the New Testament that
Jesus of Nazareth is God is blasphemy against the God
of Israel.  If the Protestant Christian would object to
having the common schools daily opened with the forms of
worship peculiar to the Catholic church, which worships
the same triune God with him, how much more serious
must be the objection of the Jew to being compelled to
attend or support the worship of a being as God, whose
divinity and supernatural history he denies?"

Suppose in a public school a Catholic teacher reads from
the apocrypha in the Douai version, 2 Maccabees, 12th
chapter, verses 44 and 45, that it was a duty to "pray for
the dead that they may be loosed from their sins"; what
view would the Protestant take of the provision in our
state constitution against sectarian instruction in our
public schools?

Under the statute the children of relator are bound to
attend some public or private school for a certain period
of each year.  Reading the Bible is an act of worship
within the meaning of the constitution, and a taxpayer
of the school district has a right to object to the reading
of the Bible in the public schools under the constitutional
provision that "no man shall be compelled to attend, erect

State v. Scheve.

or support any place of worship." *State v. Board,* 76 Wis., 177. So they have to choose between a private school and a place of worship.

The use of a public school, building for religious purposes is illegal and can be prevented upon the application of an objecting taxpayer. *Scofield v. School District,* 27 Conn., *499; *Spencer v. School District,* 15 Kan., 259; *Dorton v. Hearn,* 67 Mo., 301; *Weir v. Day,* 35 Ohio St., 143; *School District v. Arnold,* 21 Wis., 657; *State v. District Board,* 76 Wis., 177.

*Ernest O. Kretsinger, contra,* cited *Donahoe v. Richards,* 38 Me., 379; *Commonwealth v. Cooke,* 7 Am. Law Reg. [Mass.], 417; *Spiller v. Woburn,* 12 Allen [Mass.], 127; *Ferriter v. Tyler,* 48 Vt., 444; *Stevenson v. Hanyon,* 7 District Court Reports [Pa.], 585; *Vidal v. Girard's Executors,* 2 Howard [U. S.], 126, 200; *Pfeiffer v. Board of Education,* 118 Mich., 560; *Nichols v. School Directors,* 93 Ill., 61; *Millard v. Board,* 121 Ill., 297; *McCormick v. Burt,* 95 Ill., 263; *North v. Trustees,* 137 Ill., 296; *Townsend v. Hagan,* 35 Ia., 194; *Davis v. Boget,* 50 Ia., 11; *Moore v. Monroe,* 64 Ia., 367; *Nessle v. Ham,* 1 Ohio Nisi Prius, 140. Reference is also made to the letter of Hon. Samuel Maxwell commending the ruling of State Superintendent Jackson in this very affair of Freeman. Judge MAXWELL was a member of the convention that framed our constitution; and should be accepted as an authority.

The discretion of the district school board will not be interfered with by the court. *Board of Education v. Minor,* 23 Ohio St., 211.

A constitutional provision concerning religious freedom should be construed in relation to the state of the law as it existed at the time of its adoption, and the courts can take judicial notice of customs and usages in regard to the use of the Bible in public schools. *Pfeiffer v. Board of Education,* 118 Mich., 560.

The right to prescribe the general course of instruction and to direct what books shall be used must exist some-

State v. Scheve.

where. The legislature have seen fit to repose the authority to determine this in the school board. They may therefore, and rightfully, exercise it. *Donahoe v. Richards,* 38 Me., 379, 398; *Ferriter v. Tyler,* 48 Vt., 444; *Millard v. Board,* 121 Ill., 297.

A regulation of a school board requiring pupils in the public schools to learn the ten commandments and repeat them once a week, is not a violation of the constitutional guaranty of liberty of conscience and of worship. *Commonwealth v. Cooke,* 7 Am. Law Reg., 417. April, 1859.

Worship in public school is not an infringement of constitutional liberty, where pupils are neither required to take part or be present. *Moore v. Monroe,* 64 Ia., 367.

The executive department of the state of Nebraska (the department of public instruction) has constantly held that the Bible may be read and the Lord's prayer repeated in the public schools of this state. This holding has the force of law till reversed by the courts. Compiled Statutes, ch. 79, sec. 4, subdiv. 8.

Religion, morality and knowledge, however, being essential to good government, it shall be the duty of the legislature to pass suitable laws to protect every religious denomination in the peaceable enjoyment of its mode of public worship, and to encourage schools and the means of instruction. Constitution, art. 1, sec. 4.

The opinion of Judge Lyon in *State v. Board,* 76 Wis., 177, is illogical and inconsistent.

The constitutional provision was designed to secure the citizen against taxation for religious purposes, and not for the purpose of suppressing religion itself; and it does not afford a ground for enjoining religious exercises in the public school, where it appears that the burden of taxation is not thereby increased, and that plaintiff's children are not required to be present at, nor to take part in, such exercises. *Moore v. Monroe,* 64 Ia., 367.

*Franklin J. Griffen* and *Richard S. Horton,* in reply:
The rule of contemporaneous and practical construction

State v. Scheve.

relied upon by defendants in error has no application
where the constitutional provision is plain and unambigu-
ous as in the case at bar. *State v. Cornell*, 60 Nebr., 276;
*State v. Board*, 76 Wis., 177; Cooley, Constitutional Limi-
tations [6th ed.], p. 84; *Board of Education v. Minor*, 23
Ohio St., 211.

An examination of the authorities cited by the defendants in error, will show them inapplicable to the case at
bar. Not a single one of the authorities cited is under a
constitutional provision prohibiting sectarian instruction
in public schools.

*Wilbur F. Bryant* and *John H. Lindale, amici curiæ:*

We beg leave to call attention to the danger which
threatens the rights of a large body of people who constitute an important part of our citizenship, the membership
of a great church. They have the same rights as other people—no more, no less. We refer to the Roman Catholics of
Nebraska. The fact that we have church and state separated in this country is the result of a compromise. When
the constitution was formed, there were Congregationalists
in New England, Dutch Reformers in New York, Luther-
ans in New Jersey, Quakers in Pennsylvania, Catholics in
Maryland, Methodists in Georgia, Calvinists in South
Carolina, Episcopalians in Virginia, and everything and
what not in North Carolina. In order that all should be
on an equal footing, it was provided that congress should
make no law respecting an establishment of religion, or
prohibiting the free exercise thereof. This was in the first
amendment, and, with the freedom of the press and right of
petition, constituted the first article of the Bill of Rights,
as the first ten amendments are styled. Under this Bill of
Rights- -under this provision—this spirit of mutual tol-
eration gradually filtered down into the public conscience;
and the constitution of the several states adopted similar
provisions. Thus have religious denominations—all and
singular—acquired vested rights. This doctrine is the
very genius of our institutions.

State v. Scheve.

Our own state constitution provides: "All persons have
a natural and indefeasible right to worship Almighty God
according to the dictates of their own consciences. No
person shall be compelled to attend, erect or support any
place of worship against his consent, and no preference
shall be given by law to any religious society, nor shall any
interference with the rights of conscience be permitted."
Bill of Rights, sec. 4.

Compulsory education has been in force in this state
from time immemorial. It is only necessary to refer to the
act of March 30, 1901, to subdivision 16 of chapter 79 of
the Compiled Statutes of 1899, and the other links in the
chain. If the Bible is used in public schools, if hymns are
sung, and if children are compelled to attend school, you
compel attendance at a place of worship, which is contrary
to the constitution. Hymns are but prayers in metre. But
the Bible, you say, is common to all Christians. The
Catholic yields to no one in his reverence for the word of
God. In a recent editorial in the New York *Sun,* the following paragraph appears:

"As it is now, the Pope is the sole, bold, positive and
uncompromising champion of the Bible as the word of
God."

The Catholic church has condemned the so-called
"higher criticism," which is nothing but Tom Paine in a
parson's cassock. The Catholic must take his gospel
straight with no sugar-coating, or let him be anathema.
But we do not intend to have James Stuart's translation
forced down our throat without protest. It would savor of
pedantry and would serve no useful purpose to point out
the difference between the King-James version and the
Douai version. We do not ask to have the Douai edition
read in our schools; we do not think it proper. If we
should ask it, what a howl would go up all over the land—
such a howl as made the welkin ring when a nun baptized
the dying Thaddeus Stevens, at his own request—"The
arrogance of Rome!" It does make a difference whose
ox is being gored. "Orthodoxy is my doxy and heterodoxy

is your doxy," has been the song of every religious tyrant from Jew-burning Torquemada to witch-hanging Cotton Mather.

In 1854, a Know-nothing supreme court down in the state of Maine unburdened itself of the following morsel of erudition: "But reading the Bible is no more an interference with religious belief than would reading the mythology of Greece or Rome be regarded as interfering with religious belief or an affirmance of the pagan creeds." *Donahoe v. Richards,* 38 Me., 379, 399.

This is not a fair illustration. Courts are bound to know, without proof, matters of general knowledge and to take cognizance of historical facts. The gods of Olympus are back numbers; nobody believes in them. It is safe to say that, for fourteen centuries, nobody has believed in them. The difference between Homer and the Bible is the difference between a dead wire and a live wire. You can not disassociate any version of the Bible from religion. Any attempt to run the blockade under the literary flag, reminds one of Petroleum V. Nasby's definition of a conservative: "A man who takes a roundabout way to get at a devilish mean thing." In regard to the ridiculous idea that Catholic children can be evicted while the Bible is being read, it is only necessary to refer to the reasoning in *State v. Board,* 76 Wis., 177, opinion of Orton, J., pp. 219, 220.

The counsel for defendant in error had the assurance to cite *Commonwealth v. Cooke,* 7 American Law Register, o. s. [Mass.], 417, Police Court of Boston. The history of forensic effort affords no more pitiful sight than this Sisyphean attempt to elevate a piece of oracular asininity delivered by a Tombs-magistrate, to the plane of a judicial decision. This case reads like Llorente's History of the Spanish Inquisition. It all happened in the city which— the self-same year—wailed over the execution of John Brown, like Rachel weeping for her children, which shed crocodile tears over Uncle Tom's Cabin, which—five years before—had raised a mob headed by two Protestant ministers to kill a deputy United States marshal, in an abortive attempt to rescue Anthony Burns. From the maudlin mock-philanthropy and Pecksniffian hypocrisy of the sniveling, whining, senile and pharisaical Puritan, good Lord deliver us!

Counsel, for both relator and respondent, have marshalled an array of authorities which are numerically, if not substantially, formidable. There are above thirty of them in the United States, which have been cited and are recited at every coming of a case, involving this question, before a court of last resort. These authorities, in their use, are about equally divided between the sheep and the goats. Some of these are not cited by either counsel in this case.

In determining the weight of these decisions, two things are necessary: (1) A careful examination of the constitution and statute under which the decision was made; (2) a thorough sifting of *facta*—matters absolutely decided—from judicial eloquence and irrelevant *dicta* which too often befog many of the opinions.

Taking the decisions cited by counsel it will be found that in *Ferriter v. Tyler, Donahoe v. Richards, Commonwealth v. Cooke, Minor v. Board of Education, Pfeiffer v. Board of Education, McCormick v. Burt* and *Nessle v. Ham,* 1 Ohio Nisi Prius, 140; the court places the entire responsibility upon that *"quasi*-judicial" body the board of education. It is true much learning is wasted in arriving at this simple decision, but here it is in a nut-shell.

In *Scofield v. School District, Weir v. Day, School District v. Arnold, Nichols v. School Directors, Davis v. Boget, Dorton v. Hearn, Spencer v. School District* and *Townsend v. Hagan* the question is not the constitutional use of public funds, but of *ultra vires*—the power of a corporation (school district), or its officers, to divest the use of public property from the purpose of the corporation, that is, from an educational to a religious purpose. In but two of these cases is the constitutional question discussed—*Nichols v. School Directors* and *Davis v.*

62

State v. Scheve.

*Boget;* and, in each case, the court appears to have disposed of it under the maxim: *De minimis non curat lex.*

In *Spiller v. Woburn* the question really before the court was: Is the bowing of the head during prayer, an act of decorum or an act of worship?

*Millard v. Board* was decided on a question of pleading.

In *Moore v. Monroe* the court placed the responsibility with the teacher.

In *Vidal v. Girard's Executors* no such question is raised. Girard college was not a public or state school in the sense that term is used when applied to the common schools. The question concerned a charitable trust.

In *North v. Trustees* the plaintiff had forfeited all rights by his laches.

In *Stevens v. St. Mary's Training School,* 144 Ill., 336, *State v. Board* and *State v. Hallock,* 16 Nev., 973, the word "sectarian" is construed and held to be used in the popular sense as in *State v. Board, infra.*

In only seven of the cases decided (*Donahoe v. Richards, Stevenson v. Hanyon, Minor v. Board of Education, Pfeiffer v. Board of Education, Moore v. Monroe, McCormick v. Burt, Nessle v. Ham*) was the question of the use of the Bible as a text-book directly raised. The other decisions must be applied by parity of reasoning.

The decision in *State v. Board* by the supreme court of Wisconsin and Judge Moore's dissent in the *Pfeiffer Case* [Mich.] are the only instances where a court of last resort or any judge thereof had met and squarely decided the constitutional question as to the use of the Bible in public schools. The decision in Wisconsin has now been adopted by the attorneys general of two states, respectively, Minnesota and Washington, and is recognized law in those jurisdictions.

Is the Bible sectarian or literary? The pivotal question in this case is the construction of the word "sectarian." The earliest construction of the word we have been able to find, is in *Muzzy v. Wilkins,* Smith [N. H.], 1, decided in 1803; and is to the effect that the word "sect" and its

derivatives, with all distinctions thereby created and designated, relate to difference in government, discipline and
worship, but not in faith. If this definition is correct, we
are free in our confession that James's version is still a
sectarian book, as much so as the Episcopalian's.Book of
Common Prayer, the Methodist Discipline or the Lutheran
Year Book.

If King James's version of the Bible is to be used as a
literary text-book, why not enter the same plea for Vol-
taire's Candide? There are few books that exceed that immortal work in literary merit. This plea might have some
weight as to a university. But when applied to a six-year-
old child in a rural district school, it is puritanical
nonsense.

The case was argued orally by *Griffen, Horton* and *Tim-
othy J. Mahoney,* for plaintiff in error, and by *Kretsinger*
for defendant in error.

*Lindale, amicus curiœ,* did not appear. *Bryant,* being
an officer of the court, also made no oral argument.

*Mahoney:* The pivotal question is how should the terms
"sectarian instruction" (Constitution, art. 8, sec. 11),
"interference with the rights of conscience," and "place
of worship" (Constitution, art. 1, sec. 4), be construed?
To the Jew, the entire New Testament is sectarian. To
the Catholic the revealed word of God consists of tradition
or the unwritten word, and the Scriptures, all as interpreted by the church; just as to the lawyer the law of this
state consists of the unwritten, or common law, and the
statutes, all as interpreted by this court. On the other
hand it is of the essence of Protestantism to deny tradition (the common law), and to repudiate the authority of
the church (the supreme court) to interpret the Scriptures.
To read the Bible as *the* revealed word of God without authoritative note or comment is to inculcate the Protestant
idea that the Scriptures contain *all* the revealed word and
that each should be his own supreme court to interpret

them. Such inculcation amounts to instruction, and as
it is instruction according to the Protestant doctrine and
against the Catholic doctrine, it is "sectarian instruction,"
forbidden by section 11 of article 8 of the constitution.
To the Catholic it is a matter of conscience to read, with
the Scriptures, the authoritative notes and comments of
his church, and to require a Catholic pupil to take part in,
or listen to the reading of a version which he does not
accept as the Bible, and without the interpretation of his
church is an "interference with his rights of conscience"
(Constitution, art. 1, sec. 4). Such reading as a devotional exercise is an act of worship, and to compel a
Catholic child to attend such worship or a Catholic taxpayer to support such place of worship is a violation of
section 4, article 1 of our constitution.

*Kretsinger:* We insist that some copy of the Bible
ought to be read in the school. We have no objection to
the Douai version.

*  *  *  *  *  *  *  *  *  *

The Bible should be read as a masterpiece of literature;
as such King James's version is admittedly superior to the
Douai version.

The action of the relator was not at any particular
version of the Bible, but at Christianity itself—the very
foundation, ground-work and corner-stone of civilization
itself.

The genius of our institutions was not created by in-
fidels of the Freeman type, but by men who revered the
Book as the common law of our faith, the Pharos of civilization and the index to a higher, a better and a purer
life. Religion, morality and knowledge are joined together in the words of our constitution, for their better-
ment and perpetuity; it is the duty of the legislature to
encourage schools. Is it possible that in our schools and
universities Plato, Kant and Felix Adler will be welcome
guests, while Jesus of Nazareth is an outlaw? And all this
because it will not do to tread on the sensitive corns of

State v. Shreve.

Daniel Freeman? As a matter of state policy this writ should be denied. No more serious problem confronts the American people today than the proper government of our great cities. Vice, crime, degradation, want and official corruption exist to an alarming extent there.

\* \* \* \* \* \* \* \* \* \*

If the moral principles that Miss Beecher attempted to teach the pupils in her school were thoroughly taught and instilled into the minds of the youth of our cities, there would be a wonderful municipal reformation. Certainly no harm has come to the goodly city of Beatrice; civil and religious liberty exist there. If the private conscience of any man, good or bad, is allowed to dictate a school curriculum, where will this thing end?

AMES, C.

Section 4 of article 1 of the constitution of this state is as follows: "All persons have a natural and indefeasible right to worship Almighty God according to the dictates of their own consciences. No person shall be compelled to attend, erect or support, any place of worship against his consent, and no preference shall be given by law to any religious society, nor shall any interference with the rights of conscience be permitted." Section 11 of article 8 of the constitution reads as follows: "No sectarian instruction shall be allowed in any school or institution supported, in whole or in part, by the public funds set apart for educational purposes." Daniel Freeman is a resident taxpayer and a patron of the public school in school district No. 21 in Gage county. He applied for and obtained an alternative writ of mandamus running to the school board of said district, alleging that against his protest and in disregard of his objections and in opposition to his demands, the board permitted a teacher employed by them in said school to engage daily, in school hours, in the public school building in said district, and in the presence of the pupils, in certain religious and sectarian exercises, consisting of the reading of passages of her own selection from a book com-

monly known as King James's version or translation of
the Bible, and in singing certain religious and sectarian
songs, and in offering prayer to the Deity according to the
customs and usages of the so-called orthodox evangelical
churches of this country, and in accordance with the belief
and practices of such churches, the pupils joining in the
singing of such songs or hymns. The return to the writ
admitted the foregoing recited facts, except that it denied
that the exercises complained of were sectarian; but the
teacher, who was produced as a witness, admitted that she
regarded them as constituting a religious worship, and
that she conducted them solely for that reason. That they
are correctly so described there can be no doubt. Protestant sects who maintain, as a part of their ritual and discipline, stated weekly meetings, in which the exercises consist largely of prayers and songs and the reading or repeti-
tion of Scriptural passages would, no doubt, vehemently
dissent from the proposition that such exercises are not
devotional, or not in an exalted degree worshipful, or not
intended for religious edification or instruction. That
they possess all these features is a fact of such universal
and familiar knowledge that the courts will take judicial
notice of it without formal proof. That such exercises are
also sectarian in their character is not less free from doubt.
For more than three centuries it has been the boast and
exultation of the Protestants and a complaint and griev-
ance of the Roman Catholics that the various translations
of the Bible, especially of the New Testament, into the
vernacular of different peoples, have been the chief con-
troversial weapons of the former, and the principal cause
of the undoing of the latter. For the making of such
translations Wyclif, Luther, Tyndale and others have been
commended and glorified by one party, and denounced and
anathematized by the other. Books containing such translations have been committed to the flames as heretical, and
their translators, printers, publishers and distributers
persecuted, imprisoned, tortured, and put to death for par-
ticipating in their production and distribution. The sev-

State v. Scheve.

eral popular versions differ in some particulars from each
other, and all differ from the Catholic canon, both in ren-
dition of passages from which sectarian doctrines are de-
rived by construction, and in the number of books or gos-
pels, constituting what is regarded as the written record
of Divine revelation. In addition to this, there are persons
who are convinced, upon grounds satisfactory to them,
that considerable parts of the writings accepted by all Protestant denominations are not authentic, while devout
Hebrews maintain that the New Testament itself is not
entitled to a place in the true Bible. These diverse opinions have given rise to a great number of religious sects
or denominations. To some of these sects the reading in
public of any portion of any version of the Scriptures un-
accompanied by authoritative comment or explanation, or
the reading of it privately by persons not commissioned so
to do by the church, is objectionable, and an offense to
their religious feelings; to some, the utterance of public
prayer, except recitations from Scripture, is a vain and
wicked act; and to some, the songs and hymns of praise in
which others engage are a stumbling-block and an offense.

We do not think it wise or necessary to prolong a discussion of what appears to us an almost self-evident fact,
—that exercises such as are complained of by the relator
in this case both constitute religious worship and are
sectarian in their character, within the meaning of the
constitution. Nor do we feel inclined to make what might
be looked upon as a spurious exhibition of learning by
quoting at length from the many judicial decisions and
utterances of eminent men in this country concerning the
subject. Perhaps the case most nearly in point, because
of similarity both of facts involved and of constitutional
enactments construed to those in the case at bar, is *State
v. District Board,* 76 Wis., 177, 44 N. W. Rep., 967. There
are three separate and concurring opinions in this case by
three of the eminent judges of that court. The discussion
includes a thorough review of both the legal principles involved, and of the historical aspects of the controversy,

and, for the most part, and in essential particulars, voices
our own views. We think it, therefore, sufficient for our
purpose to direct attention to that authority.

But there is another matter deserving of consideration
in this connection. Secular education of children within
prescribed ages is, by a statute of this state, made compulsory. Punctuality and regularity of attendance at the
time fixed for the beginning of and throughout the daily
sessions of a district school are of first importance, both
as measures of discipline and for the development of a
trait, or the formation of a habit, of extreme importance
to the students in after-life. Very justly, and almost, if
not quite, necessarily, pupils are required to conform to
these regulations, or incur the penalty of loss of rank in
deportment and scholarship. Unless opinions of universal
acceptance in this country since the foundation of our government are at fault, it is a policy of the highest importance that the public schools should be the principal in-
struments and sources of popular education, because they
exert, more than any other institution, an influence pro-
motive of homogeneity among a citizenship drawn from
all quarters of the globe. But if the system of compulsory
education is persevered in, and religious worship or sectarian instruction in the public schools is at the same time
permitted, parents will be compelled to expose their children to what they deem spiritual contamination, or else,
while bearing their share of the burden for the support of
public education, provide the means from their own pockets for the training of their offspring elsewhere. It might
be reasonably apprehended that such a practice, besides
being unjust and oppressive to the person immediately
concerned, would, by its tendency to the multiplication
of parochial and sectarian schools, tend forcibly to the
destruction of one of the most important, if not indis-
pensable, foundation stones of our form of government.
It will be an evil day when anything happens to lower the
public schools in popular esteem, or to discourage attendance upon them by children of any class.

State v. Scheve.

The district court, without consideration of the merits of the controversy, adjudged a dismissal of the suit upon the ground that the practices complained of were so far within the discretion of the district board as not to be subject to control by mandamus. In that opinion we were—or at least the writer was—at first inclined to concur. More mature reflection has, however, convinced us that this view is erroneous. The administration of the public funds for educational purposes is entrusted solely to these boards, and the nature of their office, we think, especially enjoins upon them the duty of seeing to it that the constitutional prohibition is observed.

It may be unnecessary to remark that neither the writer nor the court is intended to be committed to any view of any of the matters of theological or exegetical controversy touched upon in the foregoing discussion. All that is intended to be said is that such matters, being the subjects of sectarian differences, are excluded by the express words of the constitution from being taught, or in any degree countenanced, in educational institutions maintained to any extent by the public funds. It is the function of the court to expound, not religious creeds or writings, but the constitution and laws of the state. We are of opinion that the return does not state facts sufficient to constitute a defense to the alternative writ, and it is recommended that the judgment of the district court be reversed, and that a peremptory writ as prayed issue from this court to the respondents and their successors in office.

DUFFIE and ALBERT, CC., concur.

By the Court: For reasons stated in the foregoing opinion, it is ordered that the judgment of the district court be reversed, and that a peremptory writ as prayed issue from this court to the respondents and their successors in office.

REVERSED.

# Appendix C

# Depredation Claim

Evidence in Support of Claim of Joseph B. Roper for depredations committed by the Chienne Sioux Arappahoes Chamanches and other confederate tribes of Indians or Indians belonging to said tribes.

Territory of Nebraska)
   Otoe County    ) SS

Canipa C. Roper & Perlina Roper each being duly sworn makes oath and says that they are now residents of Nebraska City, Otoe County, N.T. That they are of the following age to wit years that the affiants have known the Claimant Joseph B. Roper for many years last past and have lived in the family of the said Joseph B. Roper up to and prior to the 8th day of August A D 1864.

Affiants say that they know the said Roper to be a legal citizen of the United States and knows that the said Roper never aided directly or indirectly the present rebellion.

Affiants further say that they lived at the residence of the said Joseph B. Roper and in his family on the 8th day of August A.D. 1864 and know of this own knowledge passed the house or residence of Joseph B. Roper on the Little Blue river in the territory of Nebraska. that the Cheyenne, Sioux, Arappahoes, Chamanches, Kiowas, and other confederate tribes of Indians or Indians belonging to said tribes passed the house or residence of Joseph B. Roper on the little Blue river in the territory of Nebraska on the seventh day of August A D 1864 in a warlike manner.

and passed about one mile beyond the place or
residence of the said Roper & then & there
burned the house and then & there killed five
persons members of the family of the said
Eubanks. That said Indians afterwards returned to
the residence of Joseph B. Roper on the eight
day of August A D 1864 & then & there burned
the dwelling House of the said Roper & then &
there burned and destroyed & stole & carried
away all the property of the said Roper. Affiants
further say that the said Roper & family acci-
dentally saved their lives by escaping about eleven
o'clock at night on the evening of the seventh of
August A D 1864.

Affiants say that they have examined carefully
the amount of the said Joseph B. Roper which is
made a part and parcel of this affidavit and verily
believe from their knowledge of the items in the
Said account, that the Said account is true and
that the items in Said account were reasonably
worth in money at the time they were destroyed
the Sum of money charged by the Said Roper in
his Said account.

Affiants say that the dwelling House destroyed
or burned by Said Indians was a Hewed log
House built in the most Substantial & workman-
like manner & finished in good style. That Said
house contained three rooms each Seventeen feet
Square and at least eleven or twelve feet in the
clear and was in the opinion of the affiants well
worth the Sum of fifteen Hundred Dollars.

Affiants Say that Said Indians burned & destroyed, or took and carried away all the provisions Household & Kitchen furniture, clothing
books & everything owned by the Said Roper
and that the account of the Said Roper is correct
as to the items of property destroyed or burned
& stolen by the Said Indians, and that the Said
provisions, household & kitchen furniture,
clothing, books as appears by Said account were
at the time of their destruction as aforesaid by
Said Indians reasonably worth the Sum Set op-

posite to each of Said items in Said account.

Affiants say that they know that the Said Joseph B. Roper owned and had one Set of Carpenter tools and one Set of Wagon Makers tools at the time Said Indians burned & destroyed his dwelling house & other things & that Said tools were destroyed or taken away by the Said Indians. Affiants say that they believe the Carpenter tools were worth one hundred Dollars and that the wagon makers tools well worth the Sum of fifty dollars as charged in the Said account of the Said Roper.

Affiants say that they have no legal interest either direct or indirect in the claim of the Said Joseph B. Roper against the government of the United States for depredations committed by the Said Indians that affiant Canipa C. Roper is a daughter of Said Joseph B. Further affiant Saith not.

Peter Sangdon to me well known to be the identical person who Subscribed the foregoing affidavit, makes oath and says that the facts therein Stated are true and correct. I further certify that the Said Peter Sangdon is a man of integrity and truth and that his statement is entitled to full faith & credit.


Side Note No. 1—And then and there captured took and carried away the Laura Roper daughter of the said Joseph B. Roper.

Side Note No. 2—Roper & that Perlina Roper is the wife of Said Joseph

# Appendix D

# Private Note from Agnes

Le Clair. August 21st '62

DEAR COUSIN Jim
Many have been the changes since I wrote the first P. N. to you. Do you remember the first Private Note you wrote to me? This morning I went to my drawer and on picking up a letter found in it the first P. N. I received from *Cousin Jim.* You was (sic) going to Texas soon when that was written and now you are going to War. Yes Cousin Jim I shall still remember you as the same "Jim Freeman" hoping that you may pass a soldiers life pleasantly and return "all right" to your home. Then Cousin Jim you know I'll never forget you. not for a moment. I'll often think of past scenes when you and I and many others met in the Elocution Class at Morning Lecture and other places to numerous too mention! (sic) Do you think you will return soon? I trust you will but fear you will not. I can not hope you will because I do not expect it. We certainly have a "powerful army in the field." The Rebels also have a powerful army in the field. "God speed the night."

I saw a lady this week who is going to Abingdon to State Meeting. I hear of quite a number that are going—they will have a splendid meeting no doubt.

Has Cousin George gone to war? Cous. Jim I would be most happy to see you before you go to war. I need not tell you this again but I'll be content to think of the many happy hours we have spent together. This is indeed a hurried letter. You will excuse the appearance and know that I would write a good letter if I could. I will always write when I receive a letter and further will do as you request.

Write soon as you *please*

Yours Truly!

E Agnes Suiter

Jim H. Freeman
83rd Regiment
Illinois Volunteers
Monmouth

# Bibliography

*American English Geneologies;* Library of Congress, Second Ed. GPO, 1919.

Barns, Cass G. M.D., *The Sod House;* Madison, Nebr. 1867-1897.

Beatrice Daily Sun, Beatrice, Nebr., Sept. 27, 1907.

Beatrice Daily Sun, Beatrice, Nebr., Dec. 31, 1908. P. 1, C. 3 & 4.

Beatrice Daily Sun, Beatrice, Nebr. Sept. 10, 1953, P. 1, C. 6 & 7.

Beatrice Daily Sun, Beatrice, Nebr. Aug. 18, 1954, P. 5, C. 2 & 3.

Beatrice Daily Sun, Beatrice, Nebr. May 10, 1956, P. 5, C. 2 & 3.

Beatrice Daily Sun, Beatrice, Nebr. 1957, Centennial Edition.

Beatrice Daily Sun, Beatrice, Nebr. 1957, Sec. B, P. 7, C. 5.

Beatrice Daily Sun, Beatrice, Nebr. 1959.

Beatrice Daily Sun, Beatrice, Nebr. Feb. 28, 1960, P. 10, C. 1.

Beatrice Daily Sun, Beatrice, Nebr. May 18, 1960, P. 1, C. 3-6.

Beatrice Daily Sun, Beatrice, Nebr. Aug. 30, 1960, P. 6, C. 5.

Beatrice Daily Sun, Beatrice, Nebr. Jan. 7, 1962, P. 1.

Beatrice Daily Sun, Beatrice, Nebr. Jan. 26, 1962, P. 1, C. 7.

Beatrice Daily Sun, Beatrice, Nebr. May 20, 1962, P. 1, C. 6, 7, & 8.

Beatrice Daily Sun, Beatrice, Nebr. June 10, 1962, P. 3.

Beatrice Daily Sun, Beatrice, Nebr. Sept. 8, 1968, P. 7.

Beatrice Daily Sun, Beatrice, Nebr. May 5, 1968, P. 4, C. 1-4.

Beatrice Daily Sun, Beatrice, Nebr. June 2, 1968, P. 4, C. 1, 2, & 3.

Beatrice Daily Sun, Beatrice, Nebr. Oct. 9, 1969, P. 4, C. 2 & 3.

Beatrice Express, Beatrice, Nebr. April 15, 1871, P. 2, C. 4.

Beatrice Express, Beatrice, Nebr. Oct. 14, 1871, P. 3, C. 4.

Beatrice Express, Beatrice, Nebr. Jan. 13, 1872, P. 1, C. 4.

Beatrice Express, Beatrice, Nebr. Jan. 22, 1872, P. 2, C. 2.

Beatrice Express, Beatrice, Nebr. Feb. 3, 1872, P. 2, C. 4 & 5.

Beatrice Express, Beatrice, Nebr. April 20, 1872, P. 3, C. 4.

Beatrice Express, Beatrice, Nebr. Sat., April 29, 1872, P. 2, C. 3.

Beatrice Express, Beatrice, Nebr. May 4, 1872, P. 1, C. 2.

Beatrice Express, Beatrice, Nebr. June 29, 1876, P. 3, C. 3.

Beatrice Express, Beatrice, Nebr. Sept. 5, 1872, P. 3, C. 5.

Beatrice Express, Beatrice, Nebr. Feb. 27, 1873.

Beatrice Express, Beatrice, Nebr. Thur., Feb. 28, 1873, P. 2, C. 3.

Beatrice Express, Beatrice, Nebr. July 11, 1874, P. 3, C. 3.

Beatrice Express, Beatrice, Nebr. Dec. 10, 1874, P. 3, C. 4.

Beatrice Express, Beatrice, Nebr. Thurs. July 20, 1876, P. 1, C. 3.

Beatrice Express, Beatrice, Nebr. July 27, 1876, P. 3, C. 3.

Beatrice Express, Beatrice, Nebr. Aug. 24, 1876, P. 4, C. 4.

Beatrice Express, Beatrice, Nebr. Oct. 2, 1876, P. 4, C. 4.

Beatrice Express, Beatrice, Nebr. Feb. 8, 1877, P. 3, C. 3.

Beeton, Mrs. and James, A. L., M.D., *The Household Encyclopedia and Practical Home Physician,* Copyright 1883. Revised Mercantile Publishing and Advertising Company. Chicago, Ill., 1898.

Bennett, Mrs. Mary Crouse, *Diary,* 1881.

*Blue Valley Record,* Beatrice, Nebr. Wed., July 8, 1868, Vol. 1, No. 1.

*Blue Valley Record,* Beatrice, Nebr. July 16, 1868, P. 1 & 2, C. 3, 4, 5.

*Blue Valley Record,* Beatrice, Nebr. Oct. 7, 1868, P. 1, C. 3.

*Blue Valley Record,* Beatrice, Nebr. Oct. 7, 1868, P. 2, C. 8.

Chapman Brothers, *Portrait and Biographical Album of Gage County Nebraska.* Chicago, Ill. 1888.

Cleary, L. Ed.; *The Nebraska of Kate McPhelim Cleary.* Nebraska State Historical Society. 1943.

Collins, Alan C.; *The Story of America in Pictures.* Doubleday and Company, Garden City, N.Y., 1953.

*Complete Record,* District Court, Gage County, Beatrice, Nebr., Bc P. 485, 489. Be P. 38. Bc P. 311, 376.

*Complete Record,* District Court, Gage County, Beatrice, Nebr.; B 2 P. 104, 105, 202.

*Congressional Record, Senate,* U.S. Government Printing Office, 1936, Washington, D.C. P. 8390, 8391, 8392.

Cramb, L. L.; *An Appraisal of David McCanles,* Journal Printing, Fairbury, Nebr., 1968.

Dick, Everett; *The Sod House Frontier.*

Dobbs, Hugh J.; *History of Gage County Nebraska,* Western Publishing and Engraving Co., 1918.

Dubois, J. and Mathews, G.: *Galusha Grow, Father of the Homestead Law,* P. 284.

Durham, Philip; Jones, Everett L. Ed.; *The Frontier in American Literature,* Odyssey Press, N.Y., N.Y., 1969.

*Fairbury Journal,* Fairbury, Nebr. Oct. 4, 1962, P. 2, C. 3.

First Census, U.S.; Heads of Families, 1790.

Freeman, Mrs. Daniel; *Nebraska Pioneer Reminiscences,* Nebraska Historical Society.

*Freeman Genealogy,* Present Ed. Los Angeles, Calif. C. E. Birily Co. Press 1901, 52 (2) P. C. 111 U.S.; 24½ CM CN texts, Pt. 1, Early hist. Freemans in Surrey and London in England. Comp. by G. AuJou Pt. 2, Monument of. Henry Freeman, of Woodbridge, N. Jersey and some of his descendants. Comp. by T. F. Chambers, 2384, 1-10746, CS71F855, Year 1901.

*Freeman, Freeman Genealogy,* Private Ed. Boston, Mass., Franklin Press. Rand Avery and Co. 1875, 456 P. I 1; 26 CM, Comp. by Edmund Freeman of Sandwich and his descendants. Pt. 2 memorial of Samuel Freeman of Watertown and his descendants. 2383, 9-10544T, CS71.F855 Year 1875.

*Gage County Democrat,* Friday, Dec. 9, 1879, P. 1.

*Gage County Democrat,* Jan. 5, 1880, P. 3, C. 5.

*Gage County Democrat,* Aug. 1881, P. 4, C. 6.

Gibbs, Bert and Crawford, Anna Gibbs; *Diary,* 1870-1880.

Gibbs, Russell A.; *Origin of the Homestead Act.* Unpublished Report, Homestead National Monument, Beatrice, Nebr., 1942.

Gibbs, Russell A.; *United States of America to Daniel Freeman.* Unpublished Report, Homestead National Monument, Beatrice, Nebr., 1944.

Harris, George H.; *Views and Descriptions.* A Prospectus, Nebr. Historical Society Library, 1872.

Hazen, Daniel Webster; *Diary,* 1870.

*History of Nebr.;* Western Historical Co. Chicago, Ill., 1882.

*Homestead Centennial;* Beatrice, Nebr. June 1962, Souvenir Program.

*Index of the Rolls of Honor—Ancestor's Index; N.S.D.A.R.,* Vol. 1-4, B. PL, 1916.

*Index of the Rolls of Honor—Ancestor's Index: N.S.D.A.R.,* Vol. 41, 80, 1926.

*Index of the Rolls of Honor—Ancestor's Index; N.S.D.A.R.,* Vol. 81, 120, 1939.

*Index of the Rolls of Honor—Ancestor's Index; N.S.D.A.R.,* Vol. 121-160, 1940.

*Revolutionary Reference Survey*—New Hampshire, B. 17, 49. B. PL

Jaffe, Dan; *Dan Freeman,* University of Nebraska Press, 1967.

*Journal,* District Court, Gage County Nebr. Beatrice, Nebr., Book 8, P. 36.

*Journal,* District Court, Gage County Nebr. Beatrice, Nebr., Book 1, P. 401, 413, 451, 487, 514, 560.

*Journal,* District Court, Gage County Nebr. Beatrice, Nebr., Book 1, P. 406, 553, 527, 533, 569, 470.

*Journal,* District Court, Gage County, Beatrice, Nebr., B. 1, P. 36.

*Journal,* District Court, Gage County, Beatrice, Nebr. B. 1, P. 401, 413, 451, 487, 514, 56.

*Journal,* District Court, Gage County, Beatrice, Nebr. B. 1, P. 227.

*Journal,* District Court, Gage County, Beatrice, Nebr. B. 1, P. 286.

*Journal,* District Court, Gage County, Beatrice, Nebr. Bc P. 32, 115, 226.

*Journal,* District Court, Gage County, Beatrice, Nebr. Bc P. 133, Bb P. 267, 275, 353.

*Journal,* District Court, Gage County, Beatrice, Nebr. Bc P. 314, Bb P. 263, 354.

*Journal,* District Court, Gage County, Beatrice, Nebr. Bc P. 136, Bb P. 203, 364, 335, 379, 496, 554.

*Journal,* District Court, Gage County, Beatrice, Nebr. Bc P. 176, Bb P. 256, 295, 381, 399, 516.

*Journal,* District Court, Gage County, Beatrice, Nebr. Bd P. 264, Bc P. 326, 400, 325, Bd 303, 382, 452.

*Journal,* District Court, Gage County, Beatrice, Nebr. Be P. 258, Bc P. 560, Bd P. 14, 32, 297, 599.

*Journal,* District Court, Gage County, Beatrice, Nebr. Bf P. 202, Bd P. 263, 339, 376.

*Journal,* District Court, Gage County, Beatrice, Nebr. Bg P. 202.

*Journal,* District Court, Gage County, Beatrice, Nebr. Be P. 84, 85.

*Journal,* District Court, Gage County, Beatrice, Nebr. Vol. G. P. 235, 236.

*Journal,* District Court, Gage County, Beatrice, Nebr. Vol. 0, P. 216.

*Journal,* District Court, Gage County, Beatrice, Nebr. Bp P. 87.

*Journal,* District Court, Gage County, Beatrice, Nebr. Bq P. 206.

*Journal,* District Court, Gage County, Beatrice, Nebr. Br P. 32, 142.

*Journal,* District Court, Gage County, Beatrice, Nebr. Bs P. 62.

*Journal,* District Court, Gage County, Beatrice, Nebr. B 16, P. 95.

*Journal,* District Court, Gage County, Beatrice, Nebr. Bv P. 295.

*Journal*, District Court, Gage County, Beatrice, Nebr. Vol. W. P. 150, 222.

*Journal*, District Court, Gage County, Beatrice, Nebr. By P. 287.

*Journal*, District Court, Gage County, Beatrice, Nebr. Bz P. 92.

*Journal*, Supreme Court of Nebraska, 1879, P. 194-202.

Kaplan, S. David; *Personality of the First Homesteader.* Unpublished address to descendants. August 18, 1969. *Lincoln Star*, Page 1, August 19, 1969 (excerpts).

Kennedy, John F., President of the United States of America; *Presidential Documents,* title 3. The President's Proclamation 3444 Homestead Centennial year. (F.R. Doc. 62-427; Filed Jan. 10, 1962. 4:37 p.m.)

Kinnamon, Richard; *Diary,* 1875.

*The Lincoln Sunday Star,* Lincoln, Nebr. Sunday, Dec. 14, 1924. P. 1, C. 1-10. by Lulu Mae Coe.

*Lincoln Star,* Lincoln, Nebr., Jan. 27, 1935, P. 4.

*Long Beach Press—Telegram,* Long Beach, Calif., Dec. 4, 1938, By Jack Clute.

*Lincoln Journal and Star,* Lincoln, Nebr., Aug. 5, 1951, P. 2A, C. 4, 5, 6.

*The Lincoln Star,* Lincoln, Nebr. May 19, 1962, P. 3, C. 2 & 3.

*Lincoln Star,* Lincoln, Nebr. Aug. 19, 1969, P. 3, C. 1.

Marples, Charles; *Diary,* Vols. 1-2-3. Jan. 1859 to Aug. 1876.

Mattison, Roy H.; *Homestead National Monument; Its Establishment and Administration.* Reprinted from Nebraska History, Vol. 43, No. 1, March, 1962.

Mullen, Allen, Berry, Haywood, Griffith, and Dalbey; *Founders and Patriots of Nebraska.* 1935, Nebr. Hist. Society.

Muller, Edwin; *The Reconversion of Dan Freeman.* Condensed from *Future in the Reader's Digest,* Jan. 1946. P. 109-113.

National Park Service; U.S. Department of Interior, U.S. Government Printing Office, Washington, D.C., 1965, brochure homestead National Monument.

*Nebraska History Magazine,* Vol. 22, P. 75, 320, 364, 365.

*Nebraska History Magazine,* Vol. XI, No. 4, P. 190, 206.

*Nebraska History Magazine,* Vol. XIII, No. 4, P. 224.

*Nebraska Reports,* 1878-1879, Vol. 8, P. 192.

*Nebraska Reports,* Supreme Court, 1879-1880, Vol. IX.

Nicoll, Bruce, Ed.; *Nebraska Pictorial History.* University of Nebraska Press, Lincoln, Nebr., 1967.

*Norris Electric News;* Norris Rural Public Power District, Nov. 1956, Vol. 2, No. 12, P. 5 & 6.

*Omaha World Herald,* Omaha, Nebr., 1902.

*Omaha World Herald,* Omaha, Nebr., Dorris Minney, Dec. 3, 1951.

*Original Indian Depredation Claim of Joseph B. Roper,* Nebraska City, Otoe County N.T. 1864.

Peters, S. S.; *The First Homestead In The United States.* 1896. Nebr. Hist. Society.

Pinkerton, Allan; *The Spy of the Rebellion.* A. G. Nettleton & Co. Chicago, Ill., 1883.

*Record of Patent Deliveries, U.S. Land Office,* Nebraska CXLVI, 93. Found in Nebr. Hist. Society. N.S.H.S., *Plat Books* No. 25.

Sandoz, Mari; *Miss Morissa,* McGraw Hill, NY, NY, 1955.

Schmidt, Martin F. and Dee Brown; *The Settler's West.* Scribners, 1935.

Sheldon, A. E.; *Nebraska Old and New,* University Publishing Co., Lincoln, Kansas City, Dallas, N.Y., 1937.

Sheldon, Olga N. Courtesy of *Collection of the Dawson County Historical Society, Lexington, Nebr., 1860.*

Somers, W. H.; *Gage County, Its History From the First Settlement, to Present Time.* Nebr. Historical Society. Pages 10-17., 1888.

Stout, Charles; *Daniel Freeman.* Unpublished paper, Homestead National Monument, Beatrice, Nebr., 1939.

*The Beatrice Times,* Beatrice, Nebr. May 14, 1948. P. 1, C. 6, 7, & 8.

*The Bitter War Between the States,* Vol. 7, D, Davco Publishing Co., Chicago, Ill. Ed. U.S. History Society, Inc.

*The Fairbury Daily News,* Fairbury, Nebr., March 18, 1954.

*The First Homesteader;* U.S. Dept. of the Interior, Bureau of Land Management., 1862-1962.

*The Handbook of American Genealogy,* Ed. Frederick Adams Virkus, F.I. H. G. Vol. 1, 1932. Freeman, D41; F23; F35; F45; H24; 1.23.

*The Kansas City Star,* Kansas City, Mo., Sunday, Jan. 4, 1925.

*The Kansas City Times,* Kansas City, Mo., Wed., Dec. 21, 1952, P. 18, C. 3, 4, 5.

*The Nebraska Advertiser,* Brownville, Nebr. Sat., Jan. 3, 1863. P. 2, C. 1.

*The Pioneer Record,* Nebraska State History Historical Society, Lincoln, Nebr., 1896, P. 51, 52.

*Vicksburg National Military Park;* U.S. Gov't. Printing Office 1963, Washington, D.C.

Wetmore, Helen Cody; *The Last of the Great Scouts.* University of Nebraska Press, Lincoln, Nebr., 1965, 1966.

Ozanne, Minnie; Ford Times, Dearborn, Michigan, 1954. P. 30, 31.

## PERSONAL INTERVIEWS

Braucht, Linda Freeman

Bueoy, Gladys Freeman

Carpenter, C. M.

Carpenter, Mabel Carre

Davidson, Dorothy

Freeman, Maude

Freeman, Samuel

Frolick, Clara

Gearhart, Grayce

Green, Sarah

Price, Norva

Quackenbush, Agnes Freeman

Quackenbush, Charles R.

Smith, Hannah

Stapaules, Adelaide Freeman

Steele, Louis

Taylor, Verna

Wickham, Mattie

Tapes courtesy Homestead National Monument:
Clara Frolick, Samuel Freeman, Charles R. Quackenbush, D. S. Whitcomb.

Courtesy of the Freeman descendants:
Hundreds of letters, papers, and documents.